EVERYDAY ITALIAN

EVERYDAY ITALIAN

125 Simple and Delicious Recipes

giada de laurentiis

PHOTOGRAPHS BY VICTORIA PEARSON
FOREWORD BY MARIO BATALI

CLARKSON POTTER / PUBLISHERS
NEW YORK

FOR THE TWO MOST IMPORTANT MEN IN MY LIFE: my brother Dino, who was my best friend and cooking partner, and whose memory will continue to inspire me; and my adorable husband, Todd, who always encourages me to do what I love and never gets tired of Italian food.

Copyright © 2005 by Giada De Laurentiis
Photographs copyright © 2005 by Victoria Pearson
Foreword copyright © 2005 by Mario Batali

"Everyday Italian" is a servicemark of Television Food Network, G.P. Used with permission.

Published by Clarkson Potter/Publishers, New York, New York
Member of the Crown Publishing Group, a division of Random House, Inc.
www.clarksonpotter.com

CLARKSON N. POTTER is a trademark and POTTER and colophon are registered trademarks of Random House, Inc.

Printed in the United States of America

Design by Jan Derevjanik

Library of Congress
Cataloging-in-Publication Data
De Laurentiis, Giada.
    Everyday Italian : 125 simple and delicious recipes / Giada De Laurentiis.
    Includes index.
    1. Cookery, Italian.   I. Title.
    TX723.D325   2005
    641.5945—dc22   2004008663

ISBN 1-4000-5258-0

20 19 18 17

First Edition

Contents

Foreword BY MARIO BATALI

You might think that all television chefs are tight friends—that on any given night, you can find us sharing tables in four-star restaurants, indulging in six-course tasting menus with matching wines, hobnobbing with movie stars, and riding around in limousines. Or that maybe there's some sort of TV-chef club somewhere, where we meet weekly to talk about things like knives and handmade pasta. Or that we're always traveling around, hanging out in one another's kitchens, or on each other's sets, gossiping.

Not true.

I first met Giada De Laurentiis, like most of America did, by seeing her television show, *Everyday Italian*. I love the idea of watching Food Network, but in reality I rarely have time to sit back and enjoy it. Plus I'm a professional high-velocity channel surfer, and it's tough—really tough—for a show to hold my attention for more than a few seconds before I move on to some golf or MTV Cribs. But I always give Food Network a try. And one day, there was Giada, whom I'd seen doing some promotional stuff, but I'd never watched her show. She was talking about her family and antipasti, and I stuck around to see what she was about.

The first thing I noticed was that everything on the screen was beautiful—both the host and the food, which looked delicious and real and natural. Then I noticed that she really knew what she was talking about. And I realized that despite her movie-star looks, Giada isn't on television because she's merely attractive; she's a real Italian girl who can cook. I was hooked.

A few months later, I found out that Giada and I shared a friend at Food Network, and the three of us decided to make a special together—with me and Giada as cohosts. That's when I finally met her. It turns out that Giada is smart, Italian-speaking, and family-oriented—the three qualities my grandma hoped I'd find in a girl to marry. (Too late for that.) She's also a great cook, highly knowledgeable about food, and a huge amount of fun to be around—the three qualities I'd hope to find in a television partner.

And so here's her first book—like my first, about simple Italian food. Simplicity is bandied about by nearly every cookbook author under the sun, often to dubious effect. But simplicity is truly present here in *Everyday Italian*. Most of the recipes don't require more than a half-dozen ingredients or a half-page of notes, yet they still seem to cover everything I want to eat, with a determined focus to allow simple flavors to shine and an equally determined effort to get them on the table quickly (instead of spending half a day looking for ingredients, which I often have to do even when I'm cooking out of my own books). The setup of *Everyday Italian* is marvelous and easy to access, so I can find what I'm looking for without having to resort to combing through the index. And the whole book is suffused with Giada's approachable, friendly personality; not only do I want to cook the recipes in this book, I want to cook them with the author. That's what I love about a good cookbook.

Giada and I have two very separate and individual styles of Italian cooking. But both stem from a love of the same culture, the same tables, the same exquisite meals in historic spots, the same appreciation for everything that is Italian and part of our nervous system. We have approached this love, this food, this life, this passion—this everything—from opposite sides of the same coin. Her food isn't there to be made by an angry techno chef, or even someone too hung up on exactly the right thing or the new combination. Giada isn't out to impress anyone with her expertise on esoteric ingredients or her wildly inventive new flavor combinations. Her cooking is part of the twenty-first-century Italian world citizen—not a throwback to the days of handmade pasta and daylong-simmered stews. But this is still the food of grandmas and aunts and brothers and cousins and sisters and in-laws, the cooking of the real Italy, Giada's cooking, my cooking, everyone's cooking . . . this is truly the cooking of the Italian family. And this book is for everybody who wants to feed that family, every day, with great Italian food.

Introduction

I want you to have fun with this book. That's why I love cooking—it's fun. And Italian cooking is the most fun of all. It's about passion. It's about taste and smell and touch. It's about family and teamwork and togetherness, and of course it's about delicious food cooked and served at home. The heart of Italian cooking is in the home, and this book makes it easy for you to create fantastic Italian meals in your own kitchen every day of the week, whether it's a quick lunch or a Sunday dinner.

On the following pages you'll find some of the recipes I grew up with. I've updated them to simplify and streamline the cooking process without sacrificing their authentic flavor. You may have seen some of these dishes on my Food Network show, *Everyday Italian*, but until you make them yourself you won't know how wonderful they are. You don't need fancy ingredients or time-consuming techniques, just a quick trip to the supermarket and a few of my personal shortcuts. The food will be fantastic and you'll have plenty of time to enjoy your friends and family—the real reason for any Italian get-together!

I'm often asked how it happened that I cook on television. I suppose I could say it all began in Rome, where I was born, or Los Angeles, where I grew up . . . but really it all began in the kitchen. In my family, as in many Italian families, food plays a major role. Meals aren't just about eating, they are a chance for all of us to enjoy one another's company. Cooking is a communal affair and everyone takes part, even the kids. As far back as I can remember I've had fun in the kitchen, relishing the preparation of a meal as much as I love sitting down to eat it.

I'm carrying on a family tradition. My great-grandparents owned a pasta factory in Naples. My grandpa, Dino De Laurentiis, is now famous as one of Hollywood's most prolific producers, but as a boy in the 1930s he sold pasta door to door in his hometown of Naples. After he made his fortune in the film business, Nonno (Grandpa) indulged his first love by opening two Italian restaurants called DDL Foodshow here in America, one in New York and one in Beverly Hills. (They closed in the mid-1980s.) He brought over chefs from Naples, and to me they were rock stars. I hung out at the

Beverly Hills restaurant all the time when I was growing up, smelling the food, observing the chefs at work, touching everything, and sneaking a taste whenever I could! Then I'd watch the customers: the wonder on their faces as they were presented with Italian masterpieces . . . and the smiles after they ate. I was hooked.

By the time I finished high school, I knew food was my future.

I got a college degree (mostly so my parents wouldn't worry), then bought a plane ticket for Paris. Six days a week I went to culinary school, and on my one day off I wandered through the French markets. I was in heaven.

When my training was over, I came home and went to work. For years I cooked in some of California's best restaurants, from the Ritz-Carlton to Spago. Finally I struck out on my own with a catering company, GDL Foods. I also began working on magazine shoots as an assistant food stylist (the person who cooks the food that's being photographed and makes it look as appetizing as possible).

But despite my French training and my years of cooking for the rich and famous, those family dinners still served as my greatest inspiration. One day a magazine I had worked for asked me to do a story about home cooking. I got my family together for one of our traditional meals, the article was published, and before I knew it Food Network came calling.

I've been lucky enough to spend my life indulging my passion for food, and now I get to share my enthusiasm on my television show. Just as a true Italian dinner encompasses extended family, the *Everyday Italian* family includes the audience. In this book you'll find some of the recipes that viewers say they love the most and others that have never been on the show. You can be confident making all these dishes because they're simple; I believe a great meal does not have to be difficult or complex. The recipes are easy enough that you'll enjoy making them every day, but so delicious your family will ask for them again and again.

So take this book, gather your family, and have fun!

everyday

antipasti

FRESH FROM THE PANTRY

White Bean and Tuna Salad ▪ Crostini with Sun-Dried Tomatoes and Chickpeas ▪ White Bean Dip with Pita Chips

EVERYDAY SEAFOOD STARTERS

Clams Oreganata ▪ Fried Calamari

EVERYDAY FRITTATAS

Frittata with Potato and Prosciutto ▪ Frittata with Asparagus, Tomato, and Fontina Cheese

TRICOLORE

Panino alla Margherita ▪ Caprese Salad

OLIVES AND OLIVE OIL

Marinated Olives ▪ Olive and Sun-Dried Tomato Tapenade with Endive Leaves ▪ Chili-Infused Oil ▪ Pinzimonio ▪ Sweet and Spicy Roasted Almonds ▪ Rosemary-Infused Oil ▪ Popcorn with Rosemary-Infused Oil

BREAD AND SANDWICHES

Cheese and Rosemary Bread Sticks ▪ Italian Egg Sandwich ▪ Nutella Sandwich

PROSCIUTTO

Prosciutto-Wrapped Bread Sticks ▪ Roasted Asparagus Wrapped in Prosciutto ▪ Prosciutto Purses ▪ Panino di Prosciutto e Fontina

ROASTED PEPPERS

Roasted Bell Peppers ▪ Roasted Bell Pepper Salad ▪ Sweet Red Pepper Crostini

Fresh
FROM THE PANTRY

One of the keys to putting together a last-minute Italian meal—or

any meal, for that matter—that's quick, stress-free, and delicious

is to have a well-stocked pantry. Here are a few of the things I have

in mine, and on the following pages are a few dishes you can make

when you're in a hurry and there is no time to grocery shop—

that is, fresh from the pantry.

▪ **EXTRA-VIRGIN OLIVE OIL**

▪ **FRESH GARLIC**

▪ **RED PEPPER FLAKES:** If they've been in your pantry for more than six months or their color isn't a vibrant red, throw the bottle away and buy a new one. It's lost its heat.

▪ **AN ASSORTMENT OF DRIED PASTA SHAPES:** I like to have long strands such as spaghetti and linguine; short tubes like penne and rigatoni; and other shapes like shells, orecchiette ("little ears"), and farfalle (bow ties).

▪ **CANNED CANNELLINI BEANS:** These are the Italian beans also known as Tuscan white beans.

▪ **CANNED ITALIAN TUNA:** Choose meat packed in olive oil—it has more flavor.

▪ **MARINARA SAUCE:** I like to make my own (see page 59) and store it in the freezer, but you could buy your favorite jarred brand for the pantry.

▪ **DRIED HERBS:** I always have at least oregano, rosemary, thyme, and herbes de Provence.

▪ **VINEGARS:** a good balsamic for salads, and both red- and white-wine vinegars.

▪ **ONIONS:** red, Spanish, and a sweet variety such as Vidalia, as well as shallots.

▪ **CAPERS:** They add a zing to salads, sauces, meats, and fish. Available in brine or salted; I prefer the salted. The ones in brine are easier to find, though you should make sure to rinse them before using.

IN PURE OLIVE OIL
FIRST Q
NET WT. 2.8 OZ. (80g)

SOLID LIGHT TUNA
TUNA *FLOTT*
IN PURE OLIVE OIL
FIRST QUALITY
NET WT. 2.8 OZ. (80g)

SOLID LIGHT TUNA
TUNA *Fl*
IN PURE OLIVE OIL
FIRST
NET WT. 2.8 OZ. (80g)

Ingredients: tuna, olive oil, sea salt.
PRODUCT OF ITALY
Imported by:
L'ISOLA D'ORO U.S.A. INC.
TRENTON, NJ 08619

I 1698 CE
DOLPHIN SAFE

SOLID LIGH
TUN
IN PURE OL
NET WT 2

WHITE BEAN
and Tuna Salad

Throw these pantry ingredients together and you've got a terrific salad. You could add other ingredients to jazz it up, like ½ cup capers, 1 cup cherry tomatoes, and some fresh basil leaves, and you could even serve it over 2 cups fresh arugula.

4 MAIN-COURSE SERVINGS

2 (6-ounce) cans dark meat tuna, packed in olive oil

½ teaspoon sea salt, plus more to taste

½ teaspoon freshly ground black pepper, plus more to taste

2 (15-ounce) cans cannellini beans, drained and rinsed

1 medium red onion, thinly sliced

6 tablespoons red wine vinegar

IN A LARGE BOWL, add the tuna with its olive oil and ½ teaspoon each of salt and pepper. Using a fork, break up the tuna into bite-size pieces, then gently toss in the beans and onions. Drizzle with the red wine vinegar and season with more salt and pepper to taste. Transfer the salad to plates and serve.

CROSTINI WITH
Sun-Dried Tomatoes and Chickpeas

If your pantry includes a window box of fresh herbs (mine does, and I highly recommend it), you can make this recipe even more delicious by substituting fresh basil and parsley for the dried herbs. Add ¼ cup of each fresh herb when you add the sun-dried tomato, and top the finished crostini with the fresh leaves for a colorful, lively presentation to go with the great flavors.

24 APPETIZER SERVINGS

Crostini

- 1 baguette, cut into 24 diagonal slices ⅓ inch thick
- 2 tablespoons extra-virgin olive oil

Dip

- 1 large garlic clove
- 1 (15½-ounce) can chickpeas (garbanzo beans), drained and rinsed
- 3 tablespoons fresh lemon juice
- ½ teaspoon salt
- ½ teaspoon freshly ground black pepper
- ¼ cup extra-virgin olive oil
- ¼ cup oil-packed sun-dried tomatoes, drained and coarsely chopped
- 2 tablespoons dried basil leaves
- 2 tablespoons dried Italian parsley

  Lemon zest for garnish

TO MAKE THE CROSTINI Preheat the oven to 375 degrees F. Place the baguette slices in a single layer on a baking sheet, and lightly brush with oil. Toast in the oven until golden, about 8 minutes. (You can toast the bread 1 day ahead. Cool, then store airtight at room temperature.)

TO MAKE THE DIP Mince the garlic in a food processor. Add the chickpeas, lemon juice, 2 tablespoons water, salt, and pepper. Process until the mixture is almost smooth. With the machine running, gradually blend in the oil. Process until the mixture is completely smooth, scraping down the sides of the work bowl occasionally. Add the sun-dried tomatoes and dried herbs. Blend until the tomatoes and herbs are finely chopped. (The dip can be made 1 day ahead. Cover and refrigerate.) To serve, spoon 1 teaspoon of the dip on each crostini, and garnish with lemon zest or fresh herbs.

WHITE BEAN DIP WITH PITA CHIPS

This dip is the Italian version of hummus, and in my opinion it's smoother and tastier. This is a staple antipasto when I'm entertaining. The pita chips aren't Italian, but they work really well with this dip.

6 APPETIZER SERVINGS

4 pita breads, split horizontally in half

2 tablespoons plus ⅓ cup olive oil

1 teaspoon dried oregano

1½ teaspoons salt, plus more to taste

1¼ teaspoons freshly ground black pepper, plus more to taste

1 (15-ounce) can cannellini beans, drained and rinsed

¼ cup (loosely packed) fresh flat-leaf parsley leaves

2 tablespoons fresh lemon juice (from about ½ lemon)

1 garlic clove

PREHEAT THE OVEN to 400 degrees F. Cut each pita half into 8 wedges. Arrange the pita wedges evenly over a large baking sheet. Brush the pita wedges with 2 tablespoons of the oil, then sprinkle with the oregano and 1 teaspoon each of the salt and pepper. Bake for 8 minutes, then turn the pita wedges over and bake until they are crisp and golden, about 8 minutes longer.

Meanwhile, in the bowl of a food processor, combine the beans, parsley, lemon juice, garlic, and the remaining ½ teaspoon of salt and ¼ teaspoon of pepper. Pulse on and off until the mixture is coarsely chopped. With the machine running, gradually mix in the remaining ⅓ cup of oil until the mixture is creamy. Season the purée with more salt and pepper to taste. Transfer the purée to a small bowl and serve the pita toasts warm or at room temperature alongside. (The pita wedges and bean purée can be made 1 day ahead. Store the pita wedges airtight at room temperature. Cover and refrigerate the bean purée.)

Everyday
SEAFOOD STARTERS

Italians love to linger over long, multicourse meals, with a different

wine for each course and lots of time to leisurely sip it. And they

almost always start with seafood. But where Italians are likely to

prefer such first courses as an octopus salad, grilled sardines, or a

crudo of raw fish, the Italian-*American* favorites are these two

classics: baked clams and fried calamari—dishes that, unfortu-

nately, are often served greasy and soggy. The recipes that follow

produce the right result: crispy and fresh-tasting, ready for those

leisurely sips of white wine.

CLAMS OREGANATA

This is an easy yet impressive appetizer—especially perfect for a romantic evening for two. While any type of clam would work in this recipe, I use Manilas because they are hard-shelled and have less grit inside—and they are easier to find in supermarkets. But you could also use littlenecks, cherrystones, or nearly any other large or medium-size clam.

2 APPETIZER SERVINGS

½ cup plain dried bread crumbs

½ cup extra-virgin olive oil, plus extra for drizzling

2 tablespoons chopped fresh oregano

1 tablespoon chopped fresh flat-leaf parsley

1 tablespoon chopped fresh mint

½ teaspoon kosher salt

¼ teaspoon freshly ground black pepper

Coarse salt (for lining the baking sheet)

12 small Manila clams, scrubbed and shucked (shells reserved)

PREHEAT THE BROILER. In a large bowl, gently toss the bread crumbs, ½ cup of oil, all the herbs, the kosher salt, and the pepper. Be careful not to overwork the mixture. Set aside.

Line a heavy baking sheet with coarse salt and arrange 12 clam shells atop the salt. Place one clam in each shell, then top each with 2 tablespoons of the bread-crumb mixture. Drizzle with more oil. Broil until the bread-crumb topping is golden and the clams are just cooked through, about 2 minutes.

FRIED CALAMARI

Calamari *means "squid" in Italian. Italians love squid and they prepare them in lots of different ways, but one of their favorites is fried, either eaten alone or as part of a* fritto misto *(a selection of fried seafood). Below is the traditional Italian way to make them, the way I grew up eating them. It's all about the calamari itself, not about the thick, gooey coating that they are often covered with. But best of all they are super-duper easy.*

6 APPETIZER SERVINGS

Vegetable oil (for deep-frying)

2 cups all-purpose flour

2 tablespoons dried parsley

1 pound clean squid with tentacles, bodies cut into ½-inch-thick rings

2 lemons, cut into wedges

1½ teaspoons salt

1 cup Marinara Sauce (page 59), warmed

IN A LARGE, HEAVY SAUCEPAN, add enough oil to reach the depth of 3 inches and heat over a medium flame to 350 degrees F. In a large bowl, mix the flour and parsley. Working in batches, toss the squid into the flour mixture to coat. Carefully add the squid to the oil and fry until crisp and very pale golden, about 3 minutes per batch. Using a slotted spoon, transfer the fried calamari to a paper-towel-lined plate to drain.

Place the fried calamari and lemon wedges on a clean plate. Sprinkle with salt and serve with the marinara sauce.

If you don't have *a thermometer to check the oil temperature, there are two ways to test the oil. One is by dropping a small piece of bread into the oil. If it sinks to the bottom of the pan, the oil is too cold, and if it burns immediately, the oil is too hot; but if the bread sizzles slowly, the oil is just right. The other is to place the end of a wooden spoon into the oil; if the end sizzles, the oil is ready.*

FRITTATAS

A frittata is an egg-based dish that's sort of like an omelet, but simpler: Instead of folding the eggs over their fillings—which is where a lot of home cooks go wrong—you just mix everything together, and broil the top to finish cooking it. It's served firm, with the eggs completely set, and can be eaten hot or at room temperature—another factor that makes frittatas easier than omelets. ▪ As with omelets, nearly anything can go into frittatas: herbs, vegetables, meats, cheeses, and even fish. They're an especially great way to use up small amounts of leftovers, which is actually how I invent my frittata recipes: Whether it's that single stalk of fresh oregano, a few slices of prosciutto, or a small hunk of fontina, it can go in my frittata. And the results are much more often delicious than not. Here are two of my favorites—great as snacks, with a salad as a light lunch, or even as the filling for a hearty sandwich.

FRITTATA WITH POTATO
and Prosciutto

It's very European to use potatoes in omelets, tarts, and frittatas—even on pizzas. The key is to use small cubes of potato, as here, or very thin slices. You don't want to be biting into a whole mouthful of starch, and you want your potatoes to cook through in a reasonable amount of time.

6 SIDE-DISH SERVINGS

2 tablespoons olive oil

½ onion, chopped

1 (15-ounce) potato, peeled and cut into ½-inch cubes

1 garlic clove, minced

¼ teaspoon salt

¼ teaspoon freshly ground black pepper

6 large eggs

¼ cup whipping cream

¼ cup grated Parmesan cheese

2 ounces thinly sliced prosciutto, coarsely chopped

2 tablespoons chopped fresh basil

IN A 9½-INCH-DIAMETER nonstick ovenproof skillet, heat the oil over a medium flame. Add the onion and sauté until translucent, about 4 minutes. Add the potato, garlic, salt, and pepper, and sauté over medium-low heat until the potato is tender and golden, about 15 minutes.

Preheat the broiler. In a medium bowl, whisk the eggs, cream, Parmesan cheese, prosciutto, and basil to blend. Stir the egg mixture into the potato mixture in the skillet. Cover and cook over medium-low heat until the egg mixture is almost set but the top is still runny, about 2 minutes. Place the skillet under the broiler and broil until the top is set and golden brown, about 4 minutes. Using a rubber spatula, loosen the frittata from the skillet and slide it onto a plate. Cut the frittata into wedges and serve.

FRITTATA WITH ASPARAGUS,
Tomato, and Fontina Cheese

When asparagus is in season in springtime, use it to capture the flavors of the garden with a minimal amount of effort. It cooks quickly by any method—steaming, boiling, grilling, or sautéing, as here—and it's very easy to prepare. To trim asparagus of its woody stem end, simply hold one end of the spear in one hand, the other end in the other hand, and bend gently until the spear snaps—which it will do exactly where the stem starts to get woody. Asparagus has its own built-in sous chef.

6 SIDE-DISH SERVINGS

6 large eggs

2 tablespoons whipping cream

½ teaspoon salt

¼ teaspoon freshly ground black pepper

1 tablespoon olive oil

1 tablespoon butter

12 ounces asparagus, trimmed and cut into ½-inch pieces

1 tomato, seeded and diced

3 ounces fontina cheese, cubed

PREHEAT THE BROILER. In a medium bowl, whisk the eggs, cream, salt, and pepper to blend. Set aside. In a 9½-inch-diameter nonstick ovenproof skillet, heat the oil and butter over a medium flame. Add the asparagus and sauté until crisp-tender, about 2 minutes. Add the tomato and sauté 2 minutes longer. Pour the egg mixture over the asparagus mixture and sprinkle the cheese over. Cover and cook over medium-low heat until the frittata is almost set but the top is still runny, about 2 minutes. Place the skillet under the broiler and broil until the top is set and golden brown, about 4 minutes. Let the frittata stand for 2 minutes. Using a rubber spatula, loosen the frittata from the skillet and slide the frittata onto a plate. Cut the frittata into wedges and serve.

TRICOLORE

The word *tricolore* refers to the Italian flag: red, white, and green—
or, in the case of food, tomatoes, cheese, and basil. There's perhaps no better combination of flavors and textures in summertime,
when tomatoes are bursting with ripe juices and sweet basil is
readily available by the bushel, and the cool, moist texture of mozzarella is like a gust of air-conditioning for your palate. ■ By all
means, try to find freshly made mozzarella or imported buffalo-
milk mozzarella. The flavor and texture of the prepackaged stuff is
very pale in comparison. A good mozzarella—one that you're going to
eat uncooked—should be moist and springy, and should ooze milk
when you cut into it. If it's rubbery, pasty, or dry, it's just not worth it.

PANINO ALLA MARGHERITA

This sandwich made of mozzarella, tomato, and basil is my version of a BLT. It's simple, quick, and oh so yummy! The term alla Margherita *was invented in 1889 when an official from the royal palace asked a local to make pizzas for Queen Margherita. Her favorite was the one made with three toppings: tomato (red), cheese (white), and basil (green)—the* tricolore *of the Italian flag. So anything using those three toppings is known as* alla Margherita.

MAKES 1 SANDWICH

1   slice fresh mozzarella cheese (½ inch thick; about 2 ounces)

2   slices rustic white bread (each ½ inch thick)

⅛   teaspoon salt

    Freshly ground black pepper to taste

6   medium-size fresh basil leaves or 3 large

2   slices tomato (¼ inch thick)

    About 2 teaspoons olive oil

PLACE THE MOZZARELLA CHEESE atop 1 bread slice, and sprinkle with half of the salt and some pepper. Top with the basil leaves, then the tomato slices. Sprinkle with the remaining half of the salt and some more pepper, and top with the second bread slice. Brush both sides of the sandwich with the oil.

Preheat a griddle or a ridged grill pan over a medium-low flame. Grill the sandwich until the bread is golden brown and the cheese melts, pressing down with a metal spatula, about 4 minutes per side. Transfer the sandwich to a plate and serve.

CAPRESE SALAD

Every summer, we take a family vacation sailing around the Mediterranean for a couple of weeks, and inevitably we visit the incredibly beautiful island of Capri, in the Bay of Napoli. The people of Capri have coopted the classic tri-colore combination of tomato, mozzarella, and basil and called it their own: if these three ingredients define a salad, it's called Caprese. Lucky for them.

4 FIRST-COURSE SERVINGS

3 tablespoons fresh lemon juice (from about ½ lemon)

½ teaspoon salt, plus more to taste

¼ teaspoon freshly ground black pepper, plus more to taste

3 tablespoons extra-virgin olive oil

1¼ pounds assorted tomatoes (such as regular vine-ripened tomatoes, plum tomatoes, cherry tomatoes, grape tomatoes, and yellow teardrop tomatoes)

6 ounces fresh mozzarella cheese, drained and sliced

2 tablespoons thinly sliced fresh basil leaves

WHISK THE LEMON JUICE, ½ teaspoon salt, and ¼ teaspoon pepper in a medium bowl. Gradually whisk in the oil to blend. Set the dressing aside.

Cut the regular tomatoes into ¼-inch-thick slices, and the plum tomatoes into wedges. Cut the cherry, grape, and teardrop tomatoes in half. Arrange the tomatoes and cheese on a platter. Drizzle the dressing over. Sprinkle with the basil and additional salt and pepper to taste, and serve.

OLIVES AND OLIVE OIL

The fresh, fruity flavors of olives and their oils will kick the palate into high gear. Here's an easy way to tantalize your guests while you prepare the main courses: Set out a bowl of mixed olives. I love an assortment that's been marinated in herbs and oils, which you can make yourself (recipe follows); or buy prepared olives at a gourmet food shop or supermarket. You can also infuse olive oil with herbs or other flavorings, such as the Chili-Infused Oil, Pinzimonio, and Rosemary-Infused Oil in this section. Serve them with chunks of rustic bread for dipping. And then, of course, there's the whole wide world of tapenades, which have endless delicious variations. And in all of these olive and olive-oil recipes runs the undercurrent of flavors that will transport your taste buds to Italy, where olive trees adorn every landscape, and where the fruits of those trees adorn nearly every table. Make yours one of them.

MARINATED OLIVES

For a quick and extremely easy antipasto, whip up this very simple recipe. You can use any single olive variety or combination you want; some are salty and briny, some fresh-tasting, some green or black or brown, some wrinkly and pungent, some smooth and mellow. I like a simple mix of one green and one black variety. This recipe can be made one week ahead and refrigerated.

MAKES 3 CUPS

 3 tablespoons olive oil

 1 tablespoon grated lemon zest (from about 2 lemons)

 ½ teaspoon dried crushed red pepper flakes

1½ cups Sicilian cracked green olives or other green olives

1½ cups kalamata olives

 3 tablespoons fresh lemon juice (from about ½ lemon)

 2 tablespoons chopped fresh basil

IN A MEDIUM-SIZE, heavy skillet, stir the oil, lemon zest, and red pepper flakes over medium heat just until fragrant, about 1 minute. Remove from the heat and stir in the olives. Add the lemon juice and basil, and toss to coat. Transfer the olive mixture to a container. Cover and refrigerate to allow the flavors to blend, stirring occasionally, about 12 hours.

Bring the olive mixture to room temperature, stirring occasionally. Transfer the olive mixture to a small bowl and serve.

OLIVE AND SUN-DRIED TOMATO
Tapenade with Endive Leaves

This recipe is all about assembly. And when you're having people over at the last minute, having a dish like this on hand is key. You could also serve the tapenade with bread or crackers, instead of the lettuces, for a more portable snack. And tapenade can be made a day ahead, leaving you more time with your guests or family.

12 APPETIZER SERVINGS

3   (8-ounce) jars of pitted kalamata olives or cans of black olives, drained

¾   cup sun-dried tomatoes packed in olive oil

5   tablespoons extra-virgin olive oil

3   heads of endive (about ½ pound total)

6   radicchio leaves

IN THE BOWL OF A FOOD PROCESSOR, pulse the olives, sun-dried tomatoes with their oil, and the extra-virgin olive oil until well blended but still chunky. Spoon the tapenade into a serving bowl. (The tapenade can be prepared 1 day ahead. Cover and refrigerate.)

Gently remove the leaves from the endive. Wash the leaves with cold water and dry completely.

On a large platter, place the bowl of tapenade in the center. Decoratively arrange the endive leaves and radicchio around the bowl of tapenade, and serve. (The platter of tapenade, endive, and radicchio leaves can be assembled up to 8 hours ahead. Cover with plastic wrap and refrigerate.)

CHILI-INFUSED OIL

In the past few years, it's become all the rage for restaurants to serve a little saucer of olive oil, instead of butter, for diners to dip their bread in while they have the aperitivo and wait for their first courses. This simple recipe is not only great for dipping, but can also be used to liven up the flavors in other dishes—as your cooking oil, or in salad dressing, or just drizzled over grilled fish or meat. It'll keep in the fridge for a month.

MAKES ½ CUP

½ cup olive oil

1 teaspoon dried crushed red pepper

IN A SMALL, HEAVY SAUCEPAN, heat the oil and crushed red pepper flakes over a low flame, stirring occasionally, until a thermometer inserted into the oil registers 180 degrees F, about 5 minutes. Remove from the heat and let cool to room temperature, about 2 hours. Transfer the oil and pepper flakes to a 4-ounce bottle or other small container and seal the lid. Refrigerate up to 1 month.

antipasti platter *When I want to have some friends over and keep it simple and have the freedom to sit back and relax, I like to put together an antipasti platter. I start with my favorite platters (oval in shape) and arrange some Italian deli meats such as salami, prosciutto, mortadella, and bresaola. Then I add some of my favorite cheeses, such as a wedge of asiago cheese, sliced provolone cheese, sliced fontina cheese, bocconcini (bite-size mozzarella), and even an herbed goat cheese. On another platter I arrange some fresh-cut vegetables, such as carrot sticks, celery sticks, assorted bell peppers, sliced fresh fennel, and some cherry tomatoes with Pinzimonio sauce (opposite). In small separate serving bowls, I like to set out Marinated Olives (page 33), Sweet and Spicy Roasted Almonds (opposite), and Roasted Bell Pepper Salad (page 52). And to finish it off I place some fresh focaccia (you could use your favorite bread) in a basket. This way, my guests can compose their own assortment of antipasti on their plates.*

PINZIMONIO

The word pinzimonio *means "combination"—a very simple one of olive oil, salt, and pepper. It's used as a dip for raw vegetables, served as an antipasto in the summer. Try it for the refreshing Italian variation on the tired old plate of crudités with gooky dip.*

4 TO 6 APPETIZER SERVINGS

- ½ cup olive oil
- 2 teaspoons salt
- 1 teaspoon freshly ground black pepper

  Assorted cut-up fresh vegetables (such as carrots, celery, fennel bulb, radishes, red bell peppers, and cherry tomatoes)

IN A SMALL BOWL, stir the oil, salt, and pepper to blend. (The oil mixture can be made 1 day ahead. Cover and keep at room temperature.) Arrange the vegetables on a platter and serve with the dip.

Sweet and Spicy ROASTED ALMONDS

The perfect snack food—sweet and spicy and crunchy and totally satisfying. The nuts can be made two days ahead; store airtight at room temperature.

MAKES 2 CUPS

- 2 tablespoons Chili-Infused Oil (opposite)
- 1 tablespoon sugar
- 1 teaspoon kosher salt
- 2 cups blanched whole almonds

PREHEAT THE OVEN to 350 degrees F.

In a medium bowl, stir the oil, sugar, and salt to blend. Add the almonds, and toss to coat. Arrange the almond mixture on a large, heavy baking sheet, spacing the almonds evenly. Bake, stirring occasionally, until golden brown, about 15 minutes. Serve warm or at room temperature.

ROSEMARY-INFUSED OIL

This is a staple in my kitchen; it's a fantastic flavoring agent that I can use at a moment's notice. I even like to pop my popcorn in it (recipe follows). It could also be used for dipping breads or vegetables, or as the base of a salad dressing.

MAKES ½ CUP

½ cup olive oil

3 fresh rosemary sprigs (each 5 inches long)

IN A SMALL, heavy saucepan, combine the oil and rosemary. Cook over low heat until a thermometer inserted into the oil registers 180 degrees F, about 5 minutes. Remove from the heat and let cool to room temperature, about 2 hours. Transfer the sprigs to a 4-ounce bottle or another small container, then add the oil. Seal the lid and refrigerate up to 1 month.

Popcorn with ROSEMARY-INFUSED OIL

If you're tired of buttered popcorn, try a new flavor. The rosemary oil makes this version elegant and sophisticated. I love it with lots of salt.

MAKES 8 CUPS

½ cup popcorn kernels

4 tablespoons Rosemary-Infused Oil (above)

Salt

IN A LARGE, heavy pot, stir the popcorn kernels and 3 tablespoons of the rosemary-infused oil. Cover and cook over medium-high heat until the kernels have popped, shaking the pot halfway through cooking, about 3 minutes. Immediately transfer the popcorn to a large bowl. Toss the popcorn with the remaining tablespoon of oil. Sprinkle with salt to taste, and serve.

BREAD AND SANDWICHES

Sandwiches in Italy are called *panini*, but they aren't nearly as popular in Italy as they are here in the United States. Italians just don't have the same type of eat-on-the-go culture as do Americans, for whom the quick-to-prepare, quick-to-consume, ultra-portable sandwich has become a national obsession. But still, Italians do have their specialty sandwiches, and here are recipes for some of their more original varieties.

CHEESE AND ROSEMARY
Bread Sticks

I know! I know! Refrigerated dough? But this dish works beautifully as a side, and when you're making the rest of the meal from scratch this recipe will come in very handy. You can use any cheeses and herbs, but this is my favorite combination: The Parmesan and Gruyère make the bread sticks perfectly cheesy, and the rosemary gives them a hint of freshness and color. Don't tell anyone about the refrigerated dough, and they'll never know.

MAKES 2 DOZEN

⅓ cup grated Gruyère cheese or other Swiss cheese

¼ cup grated Parmesan cheese

1 teaspoon chopped fresh rosemary

1 (11-ounce) container refrigerated bread-stick dough
   (such as Pillsbury)

1 tablespoon olive oil

1 teaspoon sea salt

PREHEAT THE OVEN to 350 degrees F. Line 2 large, heavy baking sheets with parchment paper.

Chop the Gruyère cheese, Parmesan cheese, and rosemary together to mince and blend. Set the cheese mixture aside.

Separate the dough rectangles. Using a large, sharp knife, cut each dough rectangle in half lengthwise to form 2 thin strips from each rectangle. Lightly brush the oil over the dough strips. Working with one dough strip at a time, coat each strip with the cheese mixture, then roll each dough strip between your palms and the work surface into an 8-inch-long strip. Transfer the dough strips to the prepared baking sheets and sprinkle with the salt. (The bread sticks can be prepared up to this point 4 hours ahead. Cover tightly with plastic wrap and refrigerate. Remove the plastic before baking.)

Bake until the bread sticks are golden brown, about 15 minutes. Transfer the warm bread sticks to a basket and serve.

ITALIAN EGG SANDWICH

This breakfast sandwich has been passed down through our family: My grandfather used to make it with my mom, and she would make it with us. Now I'm passing it on to you.

3 teaspoons olive oil

1 large egg

⅛ teaspoon salt

Pinch of freshly ground black pepper

1 slice rustic white bread (½ inch thick)

1 garlic clove

1 tablespoon grated Parmesan cheese

¼ cup warm chunky Marinara Sauce (page 59), drained of excess liquid

IN A SMALL, heavy skillet, heat 2 teaspoons of the oil over a medium flame. Crack the egg into the skillet, and sprinkle with salt and pepper. Cover and cook until the white is firm and the yolk almost set, about 4 minutes.

Meanwhile, toast the bread until golden brown. Brush the remaining 1 teaspoon of oil over the toast. Rub the garlic over the toast, then sprinkle with the Parmesan cheese. Spoon the drained marinara sauce over the Parmesan cheese and top with the cooked egg. Serve immediately.

NUTELLA SANDWICH

Mom used to make me this sandwich for lunch, and all the kids at school wanted to trade with me. It was my absolute favorite lunch. Nutella is a chocolate-hazelnut spread that's wildly popular in Italy and is just starting to catch on here in the U.S. Give it a try and see why.

2 slices ciabatta bread (each slice ½ inch thick)

¼ cup chocolate–hazelnut spread (such as Nutella)

PREHEAT A GRIDDLE or a ridged grill pan over a medium-high flame. Grill the bread until toasted, about 2 minutes per side. Spread the chocolate–hazelnut spread over one piece of toast. Top with the second piece of toast and serve.

PROSCIUTTO

Just a decade ago, all you could expect from most deli counters was a smoked Virginia ham that tasted more salty than hammy, and had the consistency of watery meat instead of the silky-smooth texture of the best cured meats. All that has changed with the "Prosciutto Invasion," as well as the influx of great cured meat varieties from Spain and France, not to mention amazing strides in the domestic production of hams. But imported Italian prosciutto is still my favorite, and a truly fantastic way to start a meal; simply munched on its own, it's irresistible. (So *try* not to eat all of it while you're standing at the kitchen counter, reading through recipes.) And in the following pages are some of my favorite ways to dress it up for dinner: maximum flavor with minimal effort.

PROSCIUTTO-WRAPPED
Bread Sticks

I use only a few store-bought products. But this one, when wrapped in prosciutto or rolled in cheese, makes for a great-tasting and super-easy antipasto. And when you are making a large meal from scratch, a few short-cuts are always welcome. Your guests will thank you when the entrée is on time because you didn't have a meltdown trying to bake your own bread.

MAKES 2 DOZEN

1 (11-ounce) container refrigerated bread-stick dough
   (such as Pillsbury)
¼ cup grated Parmesan cheese
24 paper-thin slices of prosciutto (about 1 pound)

PREHEAT THE OVEN to 350 degrees F. Line 2 large, heavy baking sheets with parchment paper. Tear the bread-stick dough along the perforations into rectangles. Using a large, sharp knife, cut each dough rectangle lengthwise in half, forming 2 thin strips from each rectangle. Working with one dough strip at a time, coat the dough strips with the Parmesan cheese. Roll each dough strip between your palms and the work surface into a 14-inch-long strip, then transfer the dough strips to the prepared baking sheets.

Bake until the bread sticks are golden brown and crisp, about 20 minutes. Cool the bread sticks completely on the baking sheet. (The bread sticks can be prepared up to this point 8 hours ahead. Store airtight at room temperature.)

Wrap one slice of prosciutto around each cooled bread stick, arrange the prosciutto-wrapped bread sticks on a platter, and serve.

ROASTED ASPARAGUS
Wrapped in Prosciutto

This is one of those dishes that was born out of my years of catering and the necessity to come up with something new for cocktail parties. Roasting the asparagus is fast and easy and gives a lot more flavor than simply steaming.

6 APPETIZER SERVINGS

12 asparagus stalks (about 1 pound), trimmed

1 tablespoon olive oil

1 teaspoon salt

1 teaspoon freshly ground black pepper

6 paper-thin slices of prosciutto, halved lengthwise

PREHEAT THE OVEN to 450 degrees F. Peel the bottom half of each asparagus. On a heavy baking sheet, toss the asparagus with the oil, salt, and pepper. Put in the oven and roast until the asparagus is tender, about 15 minutes. Let cool completely.

Wrap each asparagus with 1 piece of prosciutto, exposing the tips. Arrange on a platter and serve at room temperature.

when buying asparagus, *you want to look for firm stems, not wilted ones, and you want the tops to be tight and closed, not like a flower whose buds have opened. These are characteristics of fresh asparagus. To trim them, all you need to do is break off the dry, fibrous ends.*

PROSCIUTTO PURSES

This is a new way to serve the classic combination of prosciutto with melon, one of Italians' famously favorite ways to start a meal. You could pierce the prosciutto purses with toothpicks to make them easier to eat. And to make the preparation easier, be sure to place the block of Parmesan in the freezer for a few minutes, so that when you shave it, it won't crumble.

MAKES 36 PIECES

2   medium cantaloupes (about 3 pounds each), halved crosswise

2   medium honeydews (about 4 pounds each), halved crosswise

36   thin slices of prosciutto (about 1½ pounds)

1   large block of Parmesan cheese (about 1 pound)

GENTLY SCRAPE OUT THE SEEDS and membranes from the cantaloupes and honeydews. Using a melon baller, scoop out balls from the flesh and place the melon balls in a large bowl. Discard the skin.

Trim the prosciutto slices into 2½-inch squares. Cover the prosciutto loosely with plastic wrap to prevent it from drying out while assembling the purses. Place one melon ball in the center of one prosciutto slice, then fold all the sides of the prosciutto over the melon ball as for a package. Place the finished purse, seam side down, on a baking sheet and cover with plastic wrap. Repeat with the remaining prosciutto squares and melon balls. (The prosciutto balls can be prepared up to this point 1 day ahead. Keep tightly covered with plastic wrap and refrigerate.)

Using a vegetable peeler and pressing firmly, shave the Parmesan into long slices (the cheese will crumble if too little pressure is used). Decoratively arrange the Parmesan slices on a large platter. Place a prosciutto purse atop each Parmesan slice and serve.

PANINO DI PROSCIUTTO E FONTINA

This is one of my favorite combinations; the salty prosciutto and creamy melted fontina cheese make my mouth water. It's amazing how grilling the sandwich brings all the ingredients together, turning an everyday sandwich into the embodiment of comfort food.

MAKES 1 SANDWICH

2 slices of fontina cheese (3 ounces total)

2 slices of rustic white bread (each ½ inch thick)

1 paper-thin slice of red onion (optional)

1 paper-thin slice of prosciutto

6 fresh baby spinach leaves

Pinch of freshly ground black pepper

About 2 teaspoons olive oil

PLACE 1 SLICE of fontina cheese atop 1 bread slice. Top with the onion, then the prosciutto and the spinach. Sprinkle with the pepper. Top with the second slice of fontina, then with the second bread slice. Brush both sides of the sandwich with the oil.

Preheat a griddle or a ridged grill pan over a medium-low flame. Grill the sandwich until the bread is golden brown and the cheese melts, pressing down with a metal spatula, about 4 minutes per side. Transfer the sandwich to a plate and serve.

ROASTED PEPPERS

Roasted bell peppers are one of the best staples to have in the fridge for helping pull together a last-minute meal or snack. They are ridiculously easy to make—in the oven, on the grill, or even over an open gas burner. They can dress up a simple green salad; serve as a condiment on a sandwich; or add texture, flavor, and color to a pasta dressing. They can be served as an antipasto with some bread or crackers, or chopped into a variety of sauces.

ROASTED BELL PEPPERS

The classic recipes for roasted pepper use just red peppers, but you can use an assortment of colors—red, orange, and yellow. Keep a close eye on the yellow variety while they cook under the broiler to ensure that they don't char; their flesh is delicate and you'll lose the beautiful yellow color.

10 red, orange, and/or yellow bell peppers

2 cups olive oil

3 garlic cloves, halved

1 teaspoon salt

1 teaspoon freshly ground black pepper

PREHEAT THE BROILER. Cover a heavy baking sheet with foil. Arrange the bell peppers on the baking sheet and broil until the skins brown and blister, turning the peppers over occasionally, about 20 minutes. Enclose the peppers in a resealable plastic bag and set aside until cooled to room temperature.

Peel and seed the peppers, and cut them into strips. In a large bowl, toss the pepper strips with the oil, garlic, salt, and pepper. Cover and refrigerate for at least 5 hours, for the flavors to blend, and up to 1 day. Bring to room temperature before serving.

ROASTED BELL PEPPER SALAD

It's easy these days to buy roasted peppers in a jar, but when making a red pepper salad (where it's all about the peppers), I take that little extra step and roast my own. Nothing beats that great fresh-roasted flavor. It's a classic antipasto dish from the Piedmont region, now popular all over Italy.

6 SIDE-DISH SERVINGS

- 2 red bell peppers
- 1 yellow bell pepper
- 1 orange bell pepper
- ⅓ cup pitted kalamata olives, quartered
- ¼ cup olive oil
- 2 tablespoons drained capers
- 6 fresh basil leaves, torn into pieces
- 4 garlic cloves, minced
- ½ teaspoon salt, plus more to taste
- ½ teaspoon freshly ground black pepper, plus more to taste

PREHEAT THE BROILER. Cover a heavy baking sheet with foil. Arrange the bell peppers on the baking sheet and broil until the skins brown and blister, turning the peppers over occasionally, about 20 minutes. Enclose the peppers in a resealable plastic bag and set aside until cooled to room temperature.

Peel and seed the peppers, and cut them into ½-inch-thick strips. In a medium bowl, toss the pepper strips, olives, oil, capers, basil, garlic, and ½ teaspoon each of salt and pepper to combine. Season with more salt and pepper to taste, and serve. (The salad can be made up to 2 days ahead. Cover and refrigerate. Bring to room temperature before serving.)

SWEET RED PEPPER CROSTINI

This is a great way to use up leftover roasted red peppers. When I and my two brothers and sister were kids, my parents often served it as an afternoon snack to ward off our hunger before dinner was ready.

MAKES 8 CROSTINI

8 slices (½ inch thick) of baguette bread

1 tablespoon olive oil

⅓ cup roasted red bell pepper strips (see page 51)

⅓ cup shredded smoked mozzarella cheese or fontina cheese

PREHEAT THE OVEN to 375 degrees F. Arrange the bread slices on a baking sheet. Brush the bread with oil and bake until the bread is pale golden and crisp, about 15 minutes. (The crostini can be prepared up to this point 1 day ahead. Cool, then store airtight at room temperature. Return the crostini to a baking sheet before proceeding.)

Preheat the broiler. Arrange the bell pepper strips atop the crostini and sprinkle with the cheese. Broil until the cheese melts, about 2 minutes. Transfer the crostini to a platter and serve immediately.

everyday

sauces

EVERYDAY TOMATO SAUCES

Marinara Sauce ▪ Tomato Sauce with Olives ▪ Checca Sauce ▪ Spicy Tomato Sauce ▪ Salsa all'Amatriciana ▪ Simple Bolognese ▪ Vodka Sauce ▪ Turkey Meatballs in Tomato Sauce ▪ Tuna and Tomato Sauce

EVERYDAY PESTOS

Basil Pesto ▪ Sun-Dried Tomato Pesto ▪ Spinach and Pine Nut Pesto ▪ Mushroom Pesto ▪ Mushroom Pesto Crostini ▪ Arugula Pesto

EVERYDAY CLASSIC SAUCES

Béchamel Sauce ▪ Mushroom Ragù ▪ Brown Butter Sauce

Everyday
TOMATO SAUCES

Even though tomatoes weren't introduced to Italy until relatively recently—they're actually a native of Peru, and were taken to Europe by Spanish conquistadores in the sixteenth century— tomato-based sauces have become the hallmark of what Americans think of as Italian food: This is "red sauce." But red sauce goes well beyond the greasy, garlic-laden stuff from the pizza parlor. The classic marinara sauce is simple and fresh, redolent with the flavors of sweet onions, carrots, and celery as well as the aromas of garlic and olive oil—but in moderation, not in the overpowering fashion of a bygone era. Remember that your tomato sauce will taste only as good as the tomatoes you put in: Although fresh tomatoes are ideal, their season is limited, and it's no small task to boil, peel, and seed them; that's not really *everyday* cooking. So I normally use the best canned ones I can find, preferably the San Marzano variety. I always have a few cans of both crushed and whole tomatoes on hand, depending on my needs. You should too.

Kick up your marinara sauce by trying my

MARINARA SAUCE

This is the basic tomato sauce that I use the most. It takes a bit of time to make, but it's worthwhile because the sauce is so versatile—and during the hour of simmering I can be doing other things out of the kitchen. So I double this recipe, freeze it, and use it all week. Store extra sauce by allowing it to cool completely, then pour two-cup portions into freezer bags and freeze for up to three months. The classic marinara sauce is great with any pasta shape. But when you're keeping it simple, why not keep it truly simple? Go with the classic spaghetti.

**MAKES ABOUT 2 QUARTS (8 CUPS);
1 QUART WILL SERVE 4 OVER PASTA AS A FIRST COURSE**

½ cup extra-virgin olive oil

2 small onions, finely chopped

2 garlic cloves, finely chopped

2 celery stalks, finely chopped

2 carrots, peeled and finely chopped

½ teaspoon sea salt, plus more to taste

½ teaspoon freshly ground black pepper, plus more to taste

2 (32-ounce) cans crushed tomatoes

2 dried bay leaves

IN A LARGE POT, heat the oil over a medium-high flame. Add the onions and garlic and sauté until the onions are translucent, about 10 minutes. Add the celery, carrots, and ½ teaspoon each of salt and pepper. Sauté until all the vegetables are soft, about 10 minutes. Add the tomatoes and bay leaves, and simmer uncovered over low heat until the sauce thickens, about 1 hour. Remove and discard the bay leaves. Season the sauce with more salt and pepper to taste. (The sauce can be made 1 day ahead. Cool, then cover and refrigerate. Rewarm over medium heat before using.)

recipe for Tomato Sauce with Olives.

TOMATO SAUCE WITH OLIVES

A great way to add just a little something extra to my basic marinara sauce.

MAKES ABOUT 1 QUART; SERVES 4 OVER A POUND OF PASTA AS A MAIN COURSE

¼ cup olive oil

1¼ cups mixed olives, pitted and halved

1½ teaspoons dried crushed red pepper flakes, plus more to taste

4 cups Marinara Sauce (page 59)

½ cup thinly sliced fresh basil

IN A LARGE SAUTÉ PAN, heat the oil over a medium-high flame. When almost smoking, add the olives and 1½ teaspoons of red pepper flakes, and sauté for 3 minutes. Reduce the heat to low, carefully pour in the marinara sauce, and simmer until the flavors blend, about 10 minutes. Stir in the basil, and season the sauce with more pepper flakes to taste. (The sauce can be made 1 day ahead. Cool, then cover and refrigerate. Rewarm over medium heat before using.)

There's just no point in making Checca Sauce at all if the

CHECCA SAUCE

My family makes this fresh, uncooked tomato sauce with cherry tomatoes. If you can't find them, substitute with any sweet tomatoes. But there's just no point in making this recipe at all if the tomatoes aren't at their peak of ripeness. This sauce is made all over Italy in the summer, when tomatoes are in season, but only in Rome is it known as alla Checca. *I like to serve it with a long, thin strand such as spaghettini or angel hair; the fresh flavors seem to go perfectly with these delicate shapes.*

MAKES ABOUT 3 CUPS; SERVES 4 OVER A POUND OF PASTA AS A MAIN COURSE

1 (12-ounce) bag of cherry tomatoes, halved

3 scallions (white and pale green parts only), coarsely chopped

3 garlic cloves

1 (1-ounce) piece of Parmesan cheese, coarsely chopped

8 fresh basil leaves

3 tablespoons olive oil

4 ounces fresh mozzarella cheese, cut into ½-inch cubes

½ teaspoon salt, plus more to taste

½ teaspoon freshly ground black pepper, plus more to taste

IN THE BOWL of a food processor, pulse the cherry tomatoes, scallions, garlic, Parmesan, basil, and oil just until the tomatoes are coarsely chopped (do not purée). Transfer the sauce to a large bowl. Stir in the mozzarella cheese and ½ teaspoon each of salt and pepper. Season the sauce with more salt and pepper to taste. Toss the sauce immediately with your choice of freshly cooked pasta.

tomatoes aren't at their peak of ripeness.

SPICY TOMATO SAUCE

The sauce known as all'arrabbiata—*or "in the angry style"—is made with hot red pepper flakes (and sometimes fresh chilies for an extra kick). I like to use the briny elements of olives and capers and skip the fresh chilies, adding depth to the spiciness rather than just more heat. Perfect with penne or rigatoni.*

**MAKES ABOUT 1 QUART;
SERVES 4 OVER A POUND OF PASTA AS A MAIN COURSE**

3   tablespoons extra-virgin olive oil

1   small onion, minced

2   garlic cloves, minced

½   cup pitted black olives, coarsely chopped

2   tablespoons drained capers, rinsed

½   teaspoon sea salt, plus more to taste

Generous pinch of dried crushed red pepper flakes

1   (28-ounce) can crushed Italian tomatoes

IN A LARGE SKILLET, heat the oil over a medium-high flame. When almost smoking, add the onion and garlic and sauté for 3 minutes. Reduce the heat to medium and add the olives, capers, ½ teaspoon of salt, and red pepper flakes, and sauté for 1 minute. Add the tomatoes and simmer until reduced slightly, about 20 minutes. Season the sauce with more salt to taste. (The sauce can be made 1 day ahead. Cool, then cover and refrigerate. Rewarm over medium heat before using.)

SALSA ALL'AMATRICIANA

This is Rome's most famous pasta sauce, but the recipe actually originated in a town outside of Rome called Amatrice. This sauce is bold and perfectly balanced with tangy tomatoes, sweet onion, and the salty meatiness of pancetta. My parents would make it for dinner on weeknights when they either didn't have a lot of time to cook or when my mom hadn't gone to the grocery store. In the time it takes to boil the water the sauce is finished. Perfect with bucatini, perciatelli, or spaghetti.

MAKES ABOUT 1 QUART; SERVES 4 OVER A POUND OF PASTA AS A MAIN COURSE

2   tablespoons olive oil

6   ounces pancetta or slab bacon, diced

1   yellow onion, finely chopped

2   garlic cloves, minced

Pinch of dried crushed red pepper flakes

1   (28-ounce) can tomato purée

½   teaspoon sea salt, plus more to taste

½   teaspoon freshly ground black pepper, plus more to taste

½   cup grated Pecorino Romano cheese

IN A LARGE, heavy skillet, heat the oil over a medium flame. Add the pancetta and sauté until golden brown, about 8 minutes. Add the onion and sauté until tender, about 5 minutes. Add the garlic and red pepper flakes and sauté until fragrant, about 30 seconds. Stir in the tomato purée, and

½ teaspoon each of salt and pepper. Simmer, uncovered, over medium-low heat until the sauce thickens slightly and the flavors blend, about 15 minutes. Stir in the cheese. Season with more salt and pepper to taste. (The sauce can be made 1 day ahead. Cool, then cover and refrigerate. Rewarm over medium heat before using.)

SIMPLE BOLOGNESE

When we were kids, this was our favorite sauce, hands down. I used to love it on everything—pasta, rice, bread, potatoes, and polenta—you name it, I covered it in bolognese. We went through a lot of it in my household. So my parents had to figure out a way to make it that was quicker than the traditional recipe, and here it is. It's just as rich and mouthwatering as the more time-consuming traditional recipe; I promise you won't know the difference. Now that I'm all grown up, I try not to use bolognese for everything, but it's tempting because it's perfect as a sauce for any type of pasta shape.

MAKES ABOUT 1 QUART; SERVES 4 OVER A POUND OF PASTA AS A MAIN COURSE

¼ cup extra-virgin olive oil

1 medium onion, minced

2 garlic cloves, minced

1 celery stalk, minced

1 carrot, peeled and minced

1 pound ground beef chuck

1 (28-ounce) can crushed tomatoes

¼ cup chopped fresh flat-leaf parsley

8 fresh basil leaves, chopped

½ teaspoon salt, plus more to taste

½ teaspoon freshly ground black pepper, plus more to taste

¼ cup freshly grated Pecorino Romano cheese

IN A LARGE SKILLET, heat the oil over a medium flame. When almost smoking, add the onion and garlic and sauté until the onion is very tender, about 8 minutes. Add the celery and carrot and sauté for 5 minutes. Increase the heat to high, add the ground beef, and sauté until the meat is no longer pink, breaking up any large lumps, about 10 minutes. Add the tomatoes, parsley, basil, and ½ teaspoon each of salt and pepper, and cook over medium-low heat until the sauce thickens, about 30 minutes. Stir in the cheese, then season with more salt and pepper to taste. (The sauce can be made 1 day ahead. Cool, then cover and refrigerate. Rewarm over medium heat before using.)

It's important to have your cream at room temperature

VODKA SAUCE

This tasty Italian-American invention (you just won't find it in Italy) looks like it's a heavy dish, but the vodka kicks in and heats up the back of your throat to cut through the heavy cream. You can buy it in a jar, but because it's a cinch to make and very yummy, it's definitely worth taking the few minutes to make it from scratch. I like to serve it with rigatoni or penne.

MAKES ABOUT 1 QUART; SERVES 4 OVER A POUND OF PASTA AS A MAIN COURSE

3 cups Marinara Sauce (page 59)

1 cup vodka

½ cup heavy cream, at room temperature

½ cup grated Parmesan cheese

½ teaspoon salt, plus more to taste

¼ teaspoon freshly ground black pepper, plus more to taste

IN A HEAVY, large skillet, simmer the marinara sauce and vodka over low heat, stirring often, until the mixture reduces by one fourth, about 20 minutes. Stir in the cream and continue to simmer over low heat until the sauce is heated through. Remove the skillet from the heat and stir in the Parmesan, ½ teaspoon of salt, and ¼ teaspoon of pepper. Season the sauce with more salt and pepper to taste.

so that it does not curdle when it is mixed with the marinara sauce.

TURKEY MEATBALLS
in Tomato Sauce

This is an Italian-American favorite, but I like to make my meatballs with turkey instead of the traditional pork, veal, and beef. It's lighter and healthier, and that way I can eat it more often. Your guests will be so busy eating them that they won't have time to ask what's in them (they are that good), especially when they adorn a gigantic family-size platter of spaghetti or linguine.

MAKES ABOUT 3 DOZEN MEATBALLS;
SERVES 4 TO 6 OVER A POUND OF PASTA AS A MAIN COURSE

¼ cup plain dried bread crumbs

¼ cup chopped flat-leaf parsley

2 large eggs, lightly beaten

2 tablespoons whole milk

¾ cup grated Romano cheese

¾ teaspoon salt

¾ teaspoon freshly ground black pepper

1 pound ground turkey, preferably dark meat

¼ cup extra-virgin olive oil

5 cups Marinara Sauce (page 59)

IN A LARGE BOWL, stir together the bread crumbs, parsley, eggs, milk, ½ cup of the cheese, and the salt and pepper. Add the turkey and gently stir to combine, being careful not to overwork the meat. Shape the meat mixture into bite-size balls.

In a large skillet, heat the oil over a medium-high flame. Working in batches, add the meatballs and cook without moving or turning the meatballs until brown on the bottom, about 3 minutes. Turn the meatballs over and brown the other side, about 3 minutes longer. Continue to cook until all the sides are golden brown. Add the marinara sauce and bring to a boil. Reduce the heat and simmer until the flavors blend, about 5 minutes. (The meatballs can be made up to this point 1 day ahead. Cool, then cover and refrigerate. Rewarm before continuing.)

Using a slotted spoon, transfer the meatballs to a serving bowl. Sprinkle with the remaining ¼ cup of cheese. Place the cooked pasta in the skillet with the remaining sauce and toss to coat. Transfer the pasta to a separate large serving bowl, and serve with the meatballs.

The meatballs *can be made ahead of time and reheated with their sauce in a 250 degree F oven for about 30 minutes. The recipe can also be used to make mini meatballs to serve as an appetizer.*

TUNA AND TOMATO SAUCE

This is another straight-from-the-pantry dish for days when there's no time to cook. My mother relied on it very heavily when I was growing up, and everyone loved it. The lemon zest wakes up all the flavors and perfumes the dish, but you could use red pepper flakes instead if you don't have a lemon.

MAKES ABOUT 1 QUART; SERVES 4 OVER A POUND OF PASTA AS A MAIN COURSE

3   cups Marinara Sauce (page 59)

2   (6-ounce) cans albacore tuna packed in oil, drained

1   tablespoon drained capers

1   teaspoon grated lemon zest (from about ½ lemon)

1   tablespoon chopped fresh flat-leaf parsley

½   teaspoon salt, plus more to taste

½   teaspoon freshly ground black pepper, plus more to taste

IN A LARGE, heavy skillet, combine the marinara sauce, tuna, capers, and lemon zest. Simmer to blend the flavors, stirring and breaking the tuna into chunks, about 5 minutes. Stir in the parsley and ½ teaspoon each of salt and pepper. Season the sauce with more salt and pepper to taste.

To serve with pasta: Add drained freshly cooked pasta to the sauce, and toss to coat. Add enough reserved cooking liquid from the pasta to moisten.

Everyday
PESTOS

Pesto is traditionally a green sauce made with pounded basil and pine nuts, but these days any uncooked sauce that's easy, quick, and puréed can be called a pesto—in fact, that's the point of it: a no-cook sauce. Pestos are not only perfect over pasta, but they're also great condiments for meats and fish, or simply spread on toasted bread as an appetizer. Fresh pesto will last three to four days in the refrigerator, stored airtight. And if you're going to be making a lot of pestos, it's likely that you're going to be using a lot of pine nuts. Store them in the freezer. Nuts can go rancid very quickly, and you don't want your expensive pine nuts turning to garbage within a matter of days. If you store them in the freezer, you can buy in bulk, save money, and always have them on hand.

To toast nuts for pesto, bake them on a cookie sheet at 400 degrees F for 5 to 10 minutes, stirring occasionally. Be sure to keep an eye on them so that they don't burn!

BASIL PESTO

The most basic, most traditional pesto is this basil-based one that was invented in Genoa, in northern Italy; it's bright green and wonderfully aromatic. Be sure to add your oil slowly, so that the sauce fully emulsifies—that is, all the ingredients bind together, creating a thick, uniform consistency. Lots of basil varieties are available, some sweeter, some spicier, and in fact basil is an important ingredient in the cooking of southeast Asia, especially in curries. Each variety will impart its unique flavor to a pesto, so be adventurous, and try whatever type appeals to you. Just remember: You need a lot of it, and it should be fresh and crisp, not wilted or soggy.

MAKES 1 CUP; SERVES 4 OVER 12 OUNCES OF PASTA AS A MAIN COURSE

- 2 cups (packed) fresh basil leaves
- ¼ cup toasted pine nuts (see page 70)
- 1 garlic clove
- ½ teaspoon salt, plus more to taste
- ¼ teaspoon freshly ground black pepper, plus more to taste
  About ⅔ cup extra-virgin olive oil
- ½ cup freshly grated Parmesan cheese

IN A BLENDER, pulse the basil, pine nuts, garlic, ½ teaspoon of salt, and ¼ teaspoon of pepper until finely chopped. With the blender still running, gradually add enough oil to form a smooth and thick consistency. Transfer the pesto to a medium bowl and stir in the cheese. Season the pesto with more salt and pepper to taste. (The pesto can be made 2 days ahead. Cover and refrigerate.)

The secret to *making pesto into a great pasta dressing is to get the sauce to the right consistency. Fresh from the food processor, pestos are usually too thick to coat pastas; you'll just end up with mounds of the sauce amid a lot of undressed noodles. You need to mix in just enough of the pasta cooking liquid to get the pesto to coat the pasta, but not so much that you've created pesto soup.*

SUN-DRIED TOMATO PESTO

In winter, when fresh tomatoes aren't at their peak of ripeness and flavor, this is a great way to get your tomato fix. Sun-dried tomatoes are a wonder ingredient: They offer the rich, sweet flavors of fresh tomatoes, but they're available year-round, they have a long pantry life, they don't take up much room, and they pack a lot of flavor into a small punch. This pesto is a great topping for sautéed or grilled fish, and it's also wonderful for a picnic because it can be eaten cold or hot. Also perfect over penne.

MAKES ABOUT 1½ CUPS; SERVES 4 OVER 12 OUNCES OF PASTA AS A MAIN COURSE

1 (8.5-ounce) jar sun-dried tomatoes packed in olive oil

1 cup (packed) fresh basil leaves

2 garlic cloves

½ cup freshly grated Parmesan cheese

½ teaspoon salt, plus more to taste

½ teaspoon freshly ground black pepper, plus more to taste

IN THE BOWL of a food processor, blend the sun-dried tomatoes and their oil with the basil and garlic just until the tomatoes are finely chopped. Transfer the pesto to a medium bowl, and stir in the cheese and ½ teaspoon each of salt and pepper. Season the pesto with more salt and pepper to taste. (This pesto will last for 1 week if stored in an airtight container.)

For this dish, *I like to use sun-dried tomatoes packed in olive oil because the oil has had time to marinate with the tomatoes, thus adding a heightened flavor to this pesto. If you can't find the oil-packed ones, then soak dry sun-dried tomatoes in extra-virgin olive oil for 12 hours.*

SPINACH AND PINE NUT PESTO

In the past few years, Americans have been treated to a dazzling array of new convenience food; the supermarket aisles are lined with items you can eat right now! I'm not a big fan of most of these. But I am a big fan of pre-washed, pretrimmed greens, like the bags of baby spinach that are almost universally available. Cleaning fresh spinach is no treat: The bunches are filled with sand and grit, requiring multiple changes of water to remove; and it's time-consuming to separate the fibrous stalks from the tender leaves. But these bags of baby spinach, on the other hand, are ready to go: Tear open the bag, dump the greens into a salad bowl, and they're ready to dress. Or just toss into the sauté pan with a little olive oil and garlic, and you can be eating bright, fresh spinach in mere seconds. Or throw into the blender with some other ingredients—and bingo! Pesto!

MAKES 1 CUP; SERVES 4 OVER 12 OUNCES OF PASTA AS A MAIN COURSE

2 cup (tightly packed) baby spinach leaves (about 2 ounces)

¼ cup toasted pine nuts (see page 70)

1 to 2 teaspoons grated lemon zest (from about 1 lemon)

2 tablespoons fresh lemon juice (from about ½ lemon)

⅓ cup olive oil

⅓ cup freshly grated Parmesan cheese

½ teaspoon salt, plus more to taste

½ teaspoon freshly ground black pepper, plus more to taste

IN THE BOWL of a food processor, combine the spinach, pine nuts, lemon zest, and lemon juice. With the machine running, gradually add the oil, blending until the mixture is creamy. Transfer the pesto to a medium bowl. Stir in the Parmesan and ½ teaspoon each of salt and pepper. Season the pesto with more salt and pepper to taste. (The pesto can be made 2 days ahead. Cover and refrigerate.)

This is great with grilled chicken.

MUSHROOM PESTO

In my family, pesto was always a green sauce. But like many people, I've stretched the definition of pesto and expanded its horizons. (That's what makes cooking so much fun.) This recipe uses a combination of dried and fresh mushrooms, both of which bring their own pronounced textures and flavors to the dish. Dried porcinis are easy to find year-round. And although they're not cheap, they're a great pantry item that you can use to jazz up a pasta dish, make a sauce to accompany a meat dish, or, of course, use as the base of this pesto.

MAKES ABOUT 1½ CUPS; SERVES 4 OVER 12 OUNCES OF PASTA AS A MAIN COURSE

1 ounce dried porcini mushrooms

8 ounces white button mushrooms, quartered

1½ cups fresh flat-leaf parsley leaves

½ cup toasted walnuts (see page 70)

2 garlic cloves

½ cup olive oil

½ cup freshly grated Parmesan cheese

½ teaspoon salt, plus more to taste

¼ teaspoon freshly ground black pepper, plus more to taste

BRING A SMALL SAUCEPAN of water to a boil. Remove the saucepan from the heat, add the porcini mushrooms, and press to submerge. Let stand until the mushrooms are tender, about 15 minutes. Drain the soaking liquid from the mushrooms and discard.

In the bowl of a food processor, combine the porcini mushrooms, button mushrooms, parsley, toasted walnuts, and garlic. With the machine running, gradually add the oil, blending just until the mushrooms are finely chopped. Transfer to a medium bowl. Stir in the Parmesan cheese, ½ teaspoon of salt, and ¼ teaspoon of pepper. Season the pesto with more salt and pepper to taste. (The pesto can be made 2 days ahead. Cover and refrigerate.)

MUSHROOM PESTO CROSTINI

Any good pesto is a great topping for toasted bread—also called crostini—but I'm especially partial to the mushroom version, which is mellower than the more herb-focused varieties.

MAKES 36 CROSTINI; 12 HORS D'OEUVRES SERVINGS

36 slices of baguette bread (each slice ½ inch thick)

¼ cup olive oil

1½ cups Mushroom Pesto (opposite)

PREHEAT THE OVEN to 375 degrees F. Arrange the bread slices on two heavy, large baking sheets. Brush the slices with the oil, and bake until the crostini are pale golden and crisp, about 15 minutes. Spoon the mushroom pesto over the crostini and serve immediately.

ARUGULA PESTO

A spicy sauce that's perfect tossed with pasta. Be sure to wash your arugula thoroughly, in at least two changes of cold water, to remove any soil and grit, which you definitely don't want in your pesto.

MAKES 1 CUP; SERVES 4 OVER 12 OUNCES OF PASTA AS A MAIN COURSE

2 cups (packed) fresh arugula

1 garlic clove

½ cup olive oil

½ cup freshly grated Parmesan cheese

½ teaspoon salt, plus more to taste

¼ teaspoon freshly ground black pepper, plus more to taste

IN THE BOWL of a food processor, blend the arugula and garlic until finely chopped. With the machine running, gradually add the oil, processing until well blended. Transfer the pesto to a large bowl, and stir in the Parmesan cheese, ½ teaspoon of salt, and ¼ teaspoon of pepper. Season the pesto with more salt and pepper to taste. (The pesto can be made 2 days ahead. Cover and refrigerate.)

CLASSIC SAUCES

Beyond the tomato-based sauces of southern Italy and the pestos

of the north, Italians all over the Boot also use what many people

think of as classic French sauces: béchamel, mushroom ragout,

and brown butter. These are endlessly versatile recipes that can

be used for pasta dressings, as condiments for meat and fish, and

as components in other dishes. They're not hard or time-consuming,

and you'll sound like a real pro when you're explaining "Oh, the

lasagna? That layer is béchamel . . ."

BÉCHAMEL SAUCE

In case you were wondering (you're probably not, actually, but I'm going to tell you anyway), this sauce is named after the Marquis de Béchamel. In Italian it's called balsamella *or* besciamella. *The original and full French version also involves steeping some onion and a bay leaf in milk for 30 minutes, to infuse the sauce with more flavor, but here's an everyday approach. My simplified version is a snap to make and is perfect with my Baked Rigatoni with Béchamel Sauce (page 115). You could also use it the way you would hollandaise sauce.*

MAKES ABOUT 4 CUPS

5 tablespoons unsalted butter

½ cup all-purpose flour

4 cups warm whole milk

½ teaspoon salt, plus more to taste

  Pinch of freshly ground white pepper, plus more to taste

  Pinch of freshly grated nutmeg, plus more to taste

IN A 2-QUART SAUCEPAN, melt the butter over medium heat. Add the flour and whisk until smooth, about 2 minutes. Gradually add the warm milk, whisking constantly to prevent any lumps from forming. Simmer over medium heat, whisking constantly, until the sauce is thick, smooth, and creamy, about 10 minutes (do not allow the béchamel sauce to boil). Remove from the heat and stir in ½ teaspoon of salt and a pinch each of white pepper and nutmeg. Season the sauce with more salt, pepper, and nutmeg to taste. (The sauce can be made up to 3 days ahead. Cool, then cover and refrigerate.)

MUSHROOM RAGÙ

If you love mushrooms, this sauce will hit the spot. You could use it as a top-ping for pastas, meats, and—my favorite—polenta. The secret to a rich, deeply flavorful sauce is to use a variety of mushrooms, preferably the wild varieties. I'm partial to cremini, oyster, and shiitake, but you could also add portobellos, hen-of-the-woods, chanterelles, or any other variety you find. The only ones I'd steer clear of are regular white button mushrooms. Their mild flavor will get lost amid the stronger tastes of the wild varieties, and their high water content will thin your sauce without providing much flavor.

MAKES ABOUT 3 CUPS; SERVES 4 OVER A POUND OF PASTA AS A FIRST COURSE

¼ cup extra-virgin olive oil

1 large onion, chopped

2 garlic cloves, minced

1 pound mixed wild mushrooms (such as cremini, oyster, stemmed shiitake), chopped

½ teaspoon salt, plus more to taste

¼ teaspoon freshly ground black pepper, plus more to taste

1 cup Marsala

2 cups reduced-sodium chicken broth

⅔ cup grated Parmesan cheese

5 fresh basil leaves

¼ cup chopped fresh flat-leaf parsley

IN A LARGE SKILLET, heat the oil over a medium flame. When almost smoking, add the onion and garlic and sauté until the onion is tender, about 8 minutes. Add the mushrooms, ½ teaspoon of salt, and ¼ teaspoon of pepper. Increase the heat to high and sauté until the mushrooms are ten-der and all the liquid has evaporated, about 8 minutes. Remove the pan from the heat and add the Marsala. Return the pan to the heat and simmer until the Marsala evaporates, about 5 minutes. Add the chicken broth and simmer until the sauce has reduced by half, about 30 minutes. Remove the pan from the heat and stir in the cheese, basil, and parsley. Season the ragù with more salt and pepper to taste. (The sauce can be made up to 2 days ahead. Cool, then cover and refrigerate. Rewarm before using.)

BROWN BUTTER SAUCE

This is the easiest sauce you will ever make and a very tasty one, but then what doesn't taste good when it's drenched in butter? This is the perfect topping for stuffed pastas like ravioli, tortellini, and agnolloti.

½ cup (1 stick) unsalted butter

6 fresh sage leaves (torn into pieces) or ¼ cup fresh basil leaves

½ teaspoon salt, plus more to taste

¼ teaspoon freshly ground black pepper, plus more to taste

Pinch of freshly grated nutmeg

⅓ cup grated Parmesan cheese

IN A LARGE, heavy frying pan, melt the butter over medium-high heat until pale golden, about 4 minutes. Add the sage or basil leaves and cook until crisp, about 2 minutes. Stir in ½ teaspoon of salt, ¼ teaspoon of pepper, and the nutmeg. Season the sauce with more salt and pepper to taste. Sprinkle with the Parmesan cheese, and serve.

The **sage leaves** are more traditional in this sauce, but I love the **basil** also. If neither of these herbs works for you, feel free to substitute your favorite herb.

everyday

pasta,

polenta,

and

risotto

FRESH FROM THE PANTRY

Lemon Spaghetti ▪ Spaghetti with Garlic, Olive Oil, and Red Pepper Flakes ▪ Orecchiette with Toasted Bread Crumbs

EVERYDAY STUFFED PASTAS

Cheese Tortellini in Light Broth ▪ Classic Italian Lasagna ▪ Individual Vegetarian Lasagnas ▪ Beef and Cheese Manicotti ▪ Pumpkin Ravioli with Sage and Toasted Hazelnuts ▪ Spinach and Mushroom Ravioli ▪ Wild Mushroom Ravioli with Basil–Pine Nut Sauce

EVERYDAY "SAUCELESS" PASTAS

Farfalle with Turkey Sausage, Peas, and Mushrooms ▪ Orecchiette with Spicy Sausage and Broccoli Rabe ▪ Pasta Primavera ▪ Ziti with Asparagus, Smoked Mozzarella, and Prosciutto ▪ Spaghetti with Clams

EVERYDAY INDULGENCES

Penne à la Carbonara ▪ Fettuccine Alfredo ▪ Baked Rigatoni with Béchamel Sauce

LEFTOVER PASTA

Pizza di Spaghetti ▪ Torta di Pasta

EVERYDAY POLENTA

Basic Polenta ▪ Fried Polenta ▪ Baked Polenta ▪ Creamy Polenta with Gorgonzola Cheese

EVERYDAY RISOTTO

Basic Risotto ▪ Wild Mushroom Risotto with Peas ▪ Risotto al Salto (Rice Cake) ▪ Arancini di Riso

Fresh

FROM THE PANTRY

If there's anything that screams "Use me straight from the pantry!," it's pasta: shelf-stable, inexpensive, universally available, and appropriate as a starter or a main course. I always have at least a few boxes around, and so I'm never at a complete loss for a meal, even when I'm feeling just too lazy to get to the market.

These recipes are among my favorites.

cooking dried pasta *It's important that you cook the pasta in an ample amount of water—6 quarts for every pound of dried pasta (which should equal about 4 servings)—so that it cooks evenly and doesn't stick together. And adding plenty of salt will help flavor the pasta; I like to use ¼ cup of sea salt. ▪ Combine the water and salt in a large pot. Cover and bring to a boil over high heat. Add the pasta and cook, stirring occasionally, until tender but still firm to the bite, about 8 minutes. (Some smaller shapes take less time, and large, thick shapes may take longer.) Drain, reserving at least ½ cup of the cooking liquid to use if needed to thin your sauce or dressing.*

LEMON SPAGHETTI

One of the easiest pasta dishes you'll ever make, this is great as a light meal or as a side dish, especially for grilled fish.

4 MAIN-COURSE SERVINGS OR 6 SIDE-DISH SERVINGS

⅔ cup olive oil

⅔ cup freshly grated Parmesan cheese

½ cup fresh lemon juice (from about 2 lemons)

¾ teaspoon salt, plus more to taste

½ teaspoon freshly ground black pepper, plus more to taste

1 pound dried spaghetti

⅓ cup chopped fresh basil

1 tablespoon grated lemon zest (from about 2 lemons)

IN A LARGE BOWL, whisk the oil, Parmesan cheese, lemon juice, ¾ teaspoon of salt, and ½ teaspoon of pepper to blend. Set the lemon sauce aside. (The sauce can be made up to 8 hours ahead. Cover and refrigerate. Bring to room temperature before using.)

Meanwhile, bring a large pot of salted water to a boil. Add the spaghetti and cook, stirring occasionally, until tender but still firm to the bite, about 8 minutes. Drain, reserving 1 cup of the cooking liquid. Add the spaghetti to the lemon sauce, and toss with the basil and lemon zest. Toss the pasta with enough reserved cooking liquid, ¼ cup at a time, to moisten. Season the pasta with more salt and pepper to taste. Transfer to bowls and serve.

SPAGHETTI WITH GARLIC,
Olive Oil, and
Red Pepper Flakes

In Italy this dish is known as aglio, olio, e pepperoncino. *It's thoroughly easy, with just one secret: Reserve some pasta water to make the sauce. My version of this dish adds fresh herbs; I've found that this combination works wonderfully, but feel free to substitute oregano, thyme, marjoram, or whichever of your favorites are fresh; dried herbs don't work in this recipe.*

4 MAIN-COURSE SERVINGS

Salt

1 pound dried spaghetti

½ cup extra-virgin olive oil

5 garlic cloves, peeled

1 teaspoon dried crushed red pepper flakes, plus more to taste

¼ cup chopped fresh flat-leaf parsley

1 tablespoon chopped fresh basil

1 tablespoon chopped fresh mint

BRING A LARGE POT of salted water to a boil. Add the spaghetti and cook, stirring often, until tender but still firm to the bite, about 8 minutes. Drain, reserving 2 tablespoons of the cooking liquid. Do not rinse the spaghetti with water; you want to retain the natural starches that help the sauce adhere to the spaghetti.

Meanwhile, in a large sauté pan, heat the oil over a medium flame. Add the garlic and sauté until golden and fragrant, about 1 minute. It's important not to overcook the garlic or else it will become bitter. Using a slotted spoon, remove and discard the garlic. Add the red pepper flakes and sauté for 1 minute. Carefully stir in the reserved cooking liquid and ½ teaspoon of salt. Immediately add the drained spaghetti and toss for 1 minute to coat well. Season with more salt and red pepper flakes to taste. Transfer the pasta to a large serving bowl. Sprinkle with the parsley, basil, and mint, and serve.

ORECCHIETTE WITH TOASTED
Bread Crumbs

Most of us think of bread crumbs as a coating for frying. But in Italian cooking, bread crumbs are also used as a main ingredient, as in this pasta dish. This recipe probably came about as a way to use up leftover stale bread—a humble inspiration for a fantastic dish. I love this dressing with orecchiette ("little ears"), but any small shape will do.

4 MAIN-COURSE SERVINGS

Salt

1 pound dried orecchiette pasta or other small-shaped pasta, such as farfalle or penne

¾ cup extra-virgin olive oil

⅔ cup Italian-style dried bread crumbs

¼ teaspoon sea salt, plus more to taste

¼ teaspoon freshly ground black pepper, plus more to taste

1 cup finely chopped prosciutto

¼ cup freshly grated Parmesan cheese

2 tablespoons fresh flat-leaf parsley, chopped

BRING A LARGE POT of salted water to a boil. Add the pasta and cook, stirring occasionally, until tender but still firm to the bite, about 8 minutes.

Meanwhile, in a large sauté pan, heat the oil over a medium-high flame. Add the bread crumbs and ¼ teaspoon each of sea salt and pepper. Stirring constantly, cook the bread crumbs until golden brown, about 2 minutes.

Working quickly, drain the pasta and stir it into the toasted bread-crumb mixture in the pan. Remove the pan from the heat and stir in the prosciutto and Parmesan cheese. Season the pasta with more salt and pepper to taste. Transfer the pasta to a large serving bowl, garnish with the parsley, and serve.

Everyday
STUFFED PASTAS

When I think of Italian-American dishes, I think of stuffed pastas—

especially baked ones like lasagna and manicotti. They're always a hit

at a party for both the guests and, just as important, the host: They

can be made in advance, leaving you free to relax and enjoy yourself. ▪

The other family of stuffed pastas are the smaller types like ravioli,

tortellini, and agnolloti. Some cookbooks provide recipes for hand-

making your own stuffed raviolis and such—making fresh pasta,

making the stuffing, then constructing each piece, then making the

sauce, then you're ready to serve. As a chef, I've made my fair share

of stuffed pastas. But it's definitely not everyday cooking—maybe in

Italy, but not here in the United States. ▪ Luckily, high-quality ready-

made stuffed pastas are increasingly available—and not just the

traditional ricotta-cheese ravioli, but those stuffed with porcini

mushrooms or lobster meat or pumpkin. You can find these in the

refrigerated sections of gourmet food shops and Italian specialty

stores, and even at better supermarkets. No need to spend all

day rolling pasta dough.

CHEESE TORTELLINI
in Light Broth

Tortellini *means "tiny cakes"; they're small pasta nuggets filled with ingredients that range from plain cheese and vegetables to meats. They're usually served at Sunday dinners, holidays (especially on Christmas Day), or on special occasions, because making them was a laborious task. But with the premade frozen stuffed pastas now available, you can make this dish in a flash any day of the week.*

4 FIRST-COURSE SERVINGS

4 cups reduced-sodium chicken broth

1 (9-ounce) package fresh cheese tortellini

½ teaspoon freshly ground black pepper, plus more to taste

3 tablespoons shredded Parmesan cheese

1 tablespoon chopped fresh flat-leaf parsley

POUR THE BROTH into a large, heavy saucepan. Cover and bring to a boil over high heat. Add the tortellini and ½ teaspoon of pepper. Cover partially and simmer over medium heat, stirring occasionally, until the tortellini are al dente, about 7 minutes. Season the broth with more pepper to taste.

Ladle the broth and tortellini into serving bowls. Top with Parmesan cheese and parsley, and serve.

Feel free to substitute your favorite stuffed tortellini or ravioli.

Classic Italian LASAGNA

Lasagna is a dish that can be made ahead and can feed a crowd; it's as easy to make for twelve as it is for four. I actually have lasagna parties where I make both the classic version and a fantastic vegetarian version (page 94), and my guests mix and match. If you make the lasagna ahead of time and serve it family style with a simple green salad as a side, you can feed a whole crowd while not spending more than five minutes in the kitchen during your party—literally, only five minutes. It can take longer just to give directions to the pizza-delivery guy.

6 MAIN-COURSE SERVINGS

Salt

2 tablespoons vegetable oil

15 dry lasagna noodles (about 12 ounces)

3 tablespoons extra-virgin olive oil

1 pound ground beef chuck

1 teaspoon freshly ground black pepper, plus more to taste

2½ cups Béchamel Sauce (page 79)

1½ cups Marinara Sauce (page 59)

1½ pounds whole-milk ricotta cheese

3 large eggs

2 tablespoons unsalted butter

2 (10-ounce) packages frozen chopped spinach, thawed and squeezed dry

3 cups shredded mozzarella cheese

¼ cup freshly grated Parmesan cheese

BRING A LARGE POT of salted water to a boil. Add the vegetable oil (the oil will help prevent the lasagna noodles from sticking together). Cook the lasagna until almost al dente, about 6 minutes (the center of the pasta should remain somewhat hard so that it won't overcook and become soggy when baked). Drain, then rinse the noodles under cold water to stop the cooking and help remove any excess starch. Cover lightly with a damp towel to prevent the pasta from drying out. Set aside.

In a large sauté pan, heat the olive oil over a medium-high flame. Add the ground beef and 1/2 teaspoon each of salt and pepper, and sauté until the beef is brown, breaking up any large clumps, about 8 minutes. Remove from the heat and drain any excess fat. Let cool completely.

Position the rack in the center of the oven and preheat the oven to 375 degrees F.

In a medium bowl, mix the béchamel and marinara sauces to blend. Season the sauce with more salt and pepper to taste.

In another medium bowl, mix the ricotta, eggs, and 1/2 teaspoon each of salt and pepper to blend. Set aside. Spread the butter over a 13 × 9-inch baking dish. Spoon one third of the béchamel–marinara sauce over the bottom of the dish. Arrange 5 lasagna noodles atop the sauce, overlapping slightly and covering the bottom of the dish completely. Spread the ricotta mixture evenly over the noodles. Top with the spinach. Arrange 5 more lasagna noodles atop the spinach, then top with the ground beef. Spoon one third of the remaining béchamel–marinara sauce over, then sprinkle with 1/2 cup of mozzarella cheese. Top with the remaining 5 sheets of lasagna noodles. Spoon the remaining béchamel–marinara sauce over the lasagna noodles, then sprinkle with the remaining mozzarella cheese and the Parmesan cheese. (The lasagna can be made up to this point 1 day ahead. Cover tightly with plastic wrap and refrigerate. Uncover before baking.)

Line a large, heavy baking sheet with foil. Place the baking dish on the baking sheet. Bake until the lasagna is heated through and the top is bubbling, about 45 minutes.

Individual Vegetarian
LASAGNAS

The beauty of a baked pasta like this is that you can really use any vegetables you want, as long as you cut them all to the same size. This version uses a lot of them, because I like the variety in textures and flavors. But if you're not a huge fan of any one of these vegetables, just omit it, and use the same quantity of another. If you prefer a simpler dish with fewer vegetables, you can do that too. It's really up to you. You can also feel free to assemble one large lasagna in a 13 × 9-inch pan from these ingredients.

6 MAIN-COURSE SERVINGS

Salt

2 tablespoons vegetable oil

1 pound fresh lasagna sheets

3 tablespoons extra-virgin olive oil

1 medium onion, finely chopped

1 large carrot, peeled and finely chopped

1 large zucchini, finely chopped

1 large yellow summer squash, finely chopped

1 bunch of asparagus, steamed and cut into ¼-inch slices

¾ teaspoon freshly ground black pepper, plus more to taste

1½ cups Marinara Sauce (page 59), or 2 cups for a large lasagna

1 (16-ounce) can white beans, rinsed and drained

2 (10-ounce) packages frozen chopped spinach, thawed and squeezed dry

2 cups shredded mozzarella cheese

½ cup freshly grated Parmesan cheese

3 tablespoons unsalted butter, cut into pieces

PREHEAT THE OVEN to 375 degrees F. Bring a large pot of salted water to a boil. Add the vegetable oil, then the lasagna sheets, and cook until almost al dente, about 4 minutes. Drain and gently rinse the lasagna sheets under cold water to stop them from cooking and to help remove any excess starch. Cover lightly with a damp towel to prevent the pasta from drying out. Set aside.

In a large skillet, heat the olive oil over a medium flame. Add the onion and sauté until soft, about 5 minutes. Add the carrot and sauté for 3 minutes. Add the zucchini and summer squash and sauté for 5 minutes. Add the asparagus and sauté for 2 minutes. Season the vegetable mixture with ½ teaspoon each of salt and pepper. Remove from the heat and let cool.

Using a 6-inch-diameter cookie cutter, cut the cooled lasagna sheets into 18 circles. Coat the bottom of each of six 6-inch gratin dishes with 1 teaspoon of marinara sauce. Place 1 pasta circle over the bottom of each dish. In a medium bowl, toss the beans with ¼ teaspoon each of salt and pepper. Arrange the beans and then the spinach over the pasta circles in the dishes, dividing equally. Top each with another pasta circle, pressing gently to compact slightly. Spoon the sautéed vegetables over the lasagnas, dividing equally, then top each with 1 tablespoon of marinara sauce. Place a third pasta circle atop each and spread each with 1 tablespoon of marinara sauce. Sprinkle with the mozzarella and Parmesan cheese, and dot with the butter. Line a baking sheet with foil and place the dishes on the prepared baking sheet. (The lasagnas can be made up to this point 1 day ahead. Cover tightly with plastic wrap and refrigerate. Remove the plastic wrap before baking.)

Bake the lasagnas until brown on top and the sauce bubbles, about 20 minutes.

Beef and Cheese
MANICOTTI

A great one-dish meal in the tradition of the classic red-checkered-tablecloth, family-owned restaurant, this is Italian-American food at its best. I like to make individual portions ahead of time, and freeze them. When I get home really late from work, I just pop one in the microwave and have a full, comforting meal in mere minutes.

6 MAIN-COURSE SERVINGS

½ pound (8 ounces) ground beef

½ cup finely chopped onion (from 1 onion)

1 (15-ounce) container whole-milk ricotta cheese

1½ cups shredded mozzarella cheese

½ cup freshly grated Parmesan cheese

2 tablespoons chopped fresh flat-leaf parsley

2 garlic cloves, minced

1½ teaspoons salt, plus more to taste

1 teaspoon freshly ground black pepper, plus more to taste

3 teaspoons olive oil

12 pieces of manicotti pasta (from one 8-ounce box)

1½ cups Marinara Sauce (page 59)

1 tablespoon butter, cut into pieces

HEAT A MEDIUM-SIZE, heavy skillet over a medium flame. Add the ground beef and onion and sauté until the meat browns and the onion is translucent, about 5 minutes. Remove from the heat, and let cool slightly.

Meanwhile, in a medium bowl, mix the ricotta, 1 cup of the mozzarella cheese, ¼ cup of the Parmesan cheese, the parsley, garlic, salt, and pepper. Stir in the meat mixture and set aside.

Brush 1 teaspoon of the olive oil over a large baking sheet. Bring a large pot of salted water to a boil. Working in batches, add the manicotti and cook until softened but still firm to the bite, about 6 minutes. Using a slotted spoon, transfer the manicotti from the pot to the prepared baking sheet and let cool.

Preheat the oven to 350 degrees F. Brush the remaining 2 teaspoons of oil over a 13 × 9 × 2-inch glass baking dish. Spoon ½ cup of the marinara sauce over the bottom of the prepared dish. Fill the manicotti with the cheese–meat mixture, and arrange the stuffed pasta in a single layer in the prepared dish. Spoon the remaining cup of sauce over the manicotti. Sprinkle the remaining ½ cup of mozzarella cheese and then the remaining ¼ cup of Parmesan cheese over the manicotti. Dot the top with the butter pieces. (The manicotti can be prepared up to this point 8 hours ahead. Cover and refrigerate.)

Bake the manicotti uncovered until it is heated through and the sauce bubbles on the bottom of the dish, about 35 minutes. Let the manicotti stand for 5 minutes and serve.

PUMPKIN RAVIOLI WITH SAGE
and Toasted Hazelnuts

Pumpkin ravioli is easier to find in the fall through the holidays, when the Halloween mascot is in season and on the minds of cooks. The sauce can also work nicely with any ravioli filling, but the pairing of pumpkin (or another sweet squash) with sage is particularly perfect, especially with the nutmeg and hazelnut flavors. This is truly a seasonal dish; to me, it tastes like autumn—even autumn in Southern California, where I'm from.

4 MAIN-COURSE SERVINGS

½ cup hazelnuts

Salt

2 tablespoons vegetable oil

1 pound fresh pumpkin ravioli

½ cup (1 stick) unsalted butter

6 fresh sage leaves, torn into pieces

Large pinch of freshly grated nutmeg

½ cup freshly grated Parmesan cheese

2 amaretti cookies (Italian macaroons)

PREHEAT THE OVEN to 350 degrees F. Place the hazelnuts on a large, heavy baking sheet, and toast in the oven, stirring occasionally, until the nuts are fragrant and light golden brown in the center, about 7 minutes. Let cool completely. Rub the hazelnuts between your palms to remove the dark skins from the nuts. In the bowl of a food processor, pulse the nuts just until they are coarsely chopped. Set aside.

Meanwhile, bring a large pot of salted water to a boil. Add the oil, then the ravioli and cook until the ravioli float to the top, about 4 minutes. Using a slotted spoon, transfer the ravioli to a large platter and tent with foil to keep warm.

In a small, heavy skillet, melt the butter over medium heat until it starts to brown, about 3 minutes. Add the sage leaves and fry until they are crisp and fragrant, about 20 seconds. Remove from the heat and stir in the nutmeg. Pour the butter sauce over the ravioli and sprinkle with the toasted hazelnuts and Parmesan cheese. Grate the amaretti cookies over the ravioli and serve immediately.

If you use ravioli with a different filling, omit the toasted hazelnuts and amaretti cookies.

Spinach and Mushroom
RAVIOLI

In this recipe I have you make ravioli from scratch—but without using fresh pasta! Don't worry, it's really not hard, and you'll look like a professional chef. Trust me.

2 MAIN-COURSE SERVINGS

¼ cup plus 4 tablespoons extra-virgin olive oil

6 ounces button mushrooms, sliced

½ teaspoon salt, plus more to taste

½ teaspoon freshly ground black pepper, plus more to taste

1 (10-ounce) package frozen chopped spinach, thawed and squeezed dry

⅓ cup freshly grated Parmesan cheese, plus more for garnish

¼ cup mascarpone cheese

¼ cup all-purpose flour (for dusting the baking sheet)

6 egg roll wrappers

1 large egg beaten with 1 teaspoon water

½ cup finely chopped assorted mushrooms (such as cremini, button, and stemmed shiitake)

2½ cups Marinara Sauce (page 59)

IN A LARGE SAUTÉ PAN, heat ¼ cup of oil over a medium-high flame. Add the sliced button mushrooms and sprinkle with ½ teaspoon each of salt and pepper. Sauté until the liquid has evaporated from the mushrooms, about 6 minutes. Add the spinach and sauté for 2 minutes. Transfer the mixture to the bowl of a food processor. Pulse until a coarse texture forms. Transfer the spinach mixture to a large bowl and stir in ⅓ cup of Parmesan cheese and the mascarpone. Season the filling with more salt and pepper to taste.

Lightly flour a baking sheet. Arrange 3 egg roll wrappers on a cutting board. Brush with the egg and water mixture. Using a tablespoon, spoon 4 mounds of the spinach mixture 1 inch apart on each wrapper, forming 2 mounds on the first row and 2 mounds on the second. Top each with another wrapper and press around the filling to seal the edges. Using a fluted ravioli cutter, cut out the ravioli squares, forming 12 total. Place the ravioli on the prepared baking sheet and cover with a clean towel.

In a large, heavy sauté pan, heat 2 tablespoons of oil over a medium-high flame. Add the chopped assorted mushrooms and sauté until soft and most of the liquid has evaporated, about 8 minutes. Carefully stir in the marinara sauce and simmer for 5 minutes. Season the mushroom sauce with more salt and pepper to taste.

Bring a large pot of salted water to a boil. Add the remaining 2 table-spoons of oil. Adding 4 ravioli at a time to the boiling salted water, cook the ravioli until tender, about 3 minutes (working in small batches will prevent the ravioli from crowding in the pot and sticking together). Using a slotted spoon, transfer the ravioli to 2 plates. Spoon the mush-room sauce over the ravioli, sprinkle with Parmesan cheese, and serve immediately.

I like to double this recipe *and freeze the uncooked ravioli. To make sure they don't stick together, line a cookie sheet with either wax paper or plastic wrap, arrange a single layer of ravioli on the sheet, freeze for 15 minutes, and then place them into a resealable plastic bag and store in the freezer. When you are ready to serve, toss the frozen ravioli into boiling salted and oiled water and cook for 3 minutes.*

WILD MUSHROOM RAVIOLI
with Basil–Pine Nut Sauce

Wild mushroom ravioli are my very favorites, so I always have a box of them in my freezer. In the time it takes the water to boil and the raviolis to cook— no need to thaw or defrost them—I can make this sauce, and have this great dish on the table in a flash.

4 MAIN-COURSE SERVINGS

3   tablespoons pine nuts

    Salt

1   (11-ounce) package fresh wild mushroom ravioli

½   cup (1 stick) unsalted butter

¼   cup fresh basil leaves

¼   teaspoon freshly ground black pepper, plus more to taste

    Pinch of freshly grated nutmeg

⅓   cup freshly grated Parmesan cheese

PREHEAT THE OVEN to 350 degrees F. Place the pine nuts on a heavy baking sheet, and toast in the oven until the nuts are fragrant and light golden brown in the center, about 7 minutes. Let cool.

Bring a large pot of salted water to a boil. Add the ravioli and boil until they are just cooked through, stirring occasionally, about 5 minutes. Drain.

Meanwhile, in a large, heavy frying pan, melt the butter over medium-high heat until pale golden, about 4 minutes. Add the basil leaves and cook until crisp, about 2 minutes. Stir in ½ teaspoon of salt, ¼ teaspoon of pepper, and the nutmeg. Season the sauce with more salt and pepper to taste. Add the cooked ravioli, and gently toss to coat. Divide the ravioli among 4 plates and sprinkle with the Parmesan cheese and pine nuts, and serve.

"SAUCELESS" PASTAS

In the United States, we eat a lot of heavily sauced pastas. But in Italy, you're just as likely to find pasta in a light dressing as swimming in a pool of sauce; Italians like pasta dishes in which the texture and flavor of the pasta are just as important as the accompaniment. ▪ The key to most of these "sauceless" dressings is the pasta cooking water. Do not pour it all down the drain! The following recipes all use the salty, slightly starchy cooking liquid as a base and binder for other simple ingredients to create a highly flavorful sauce that lets you really enjoy what can be best about pasta dishes: the pasta. ▪ And even a lot of tomato-based sauces could use a little thinning. I think one of the most common mistakes made by home cooks is to serve their sauces too thick. The answer is to reserve a little of the pasta cooking liquid, and to add that liquid to whatever sauce you've made. Try it, and you'll be amazed at what a difference this simple trick makes.

FARFALLE WITH TURKEY SAUSAGE,
Peas, and Mushrooms

Traditionally, this dish is made with pork sausage. But in an effort to lighten things up, I use turkey sausage, which in general is a great, healthy alternative to pork. I promise that you won't be able to tell the difference.

4 MAIN-COURSE SERVINGS

½ cup extra-virgin olive oil

1 pound Italian-style turkey sausages, casings removed

10 ounces cremini mushrooms, sliced

¾ teaspoon sea salt, plus more to taste

¾ teaspoon freshly ground black pepper, plus more to taste

1 (10-ounce) package frozen peas, defrosted slightly

1 pound dried farfalle pasta (bow-tie pasta)

½ cup freshly grated Parmesan cheese

IN A LARGE SAUTÉ PAN, heat 2 tablespoons of the oil over a high flame. Add the turkey sausage and sauté until golden brown, breaking up any large clumps, about 5 minutes. Using a slotted spoon, transfer the sausage to a plate and set aside. Heat 2 more tablespoons of oil in the same pan. Add the mushrooms and ½ teaspoon each of salt and pepper. Sauté until all the liquid from the mushrooms has evaporated, about 8 minutes. Add the peas and sauté for 2 minutes. Return the sausage to the pan and cook until the sausage is heated through and the flavors have blended, about 3 minutes.

Meanwhile, bring a large pot of salted water to a boil. Add the farfalle and cook, stirring occasionally, until al dente, about 8 minutes. Drain the pasta, reserving ½ cup of the cooking water. Return the pasta to the pot and add the meat mixture. Toss over medium heat to combine and heat through, adding enough of the reserved cooking water to moisten, about 5 minutes. Drizzle in the remaining oil. Season the pasta with more salt and pepper to taste. Remove the pan from the heat. Add the Parmesan cheese and toss to combine. Transfer the pasta mixture to a large bowl and serve.

ORECCHIETTE WITH SPICY SAUSAGE
and Broccoli Rabe

This recipe is a prime example that you don't need tomato sauce to make a great-tasting pasta dish. And here's a bonus: It tastes great at room temperature, so it's perfect for picnics and casual buffet lunches.

4 MAIN-COURSE SERVINGS

Salt

2 bunches of broccoli rabe, stalks trimmed and quartered crosswise

12 ounces dried orecchiette pasta or other small shaped pasta, such as farfalle or penne

3 tablespoons olive oil

1 pound spicy pork sausage, casings removed

3 garlic cloves, minced

Pinch of dried crushed red pepper flakes

¼ cup freshly grated Parmesan cheese

½ teaspoon freshly ground black pepper

BRING A LARGE POT of salted water to a boil. Add the broccoli rabe and cook until crisp-tender, about 1 minute. Strain the broccoli rabe, reserving all the cooking liquid. Set the broccoli rabe aside. Cook the orecchiette in the same pot of boiling salted water until tender but still firm to the bite, stirring occasionally, about 8 minutes. Drain, reserving 1 cup of the cooking liquid.

Meanwhile, in a large, heavy skillet, heat the oil over a medium flame. Add the sausage and cook, breaking up with a spoon, until the sausage is brown and juices form, about 8 minutes. Add the garlic and red pepper flakes, and sauté until fragrant, about 30 seconds. Add the broccoli rabe and toss to coat. Add the pasta and enough reserved cooking liquid, ¼ cup at a time, to moisten. Stir the Parmesan cheese, salt to taste, and pepper into the pasta mixture. Transfer to pasta bowls and serve.

PASTA PRIMAVERA

Primavera is Italian for "spring," and that's what this dish tastes like. It was created at Le Cirque, New York's famed restaurant, in the 1970s because some high-flying and health-conscious patrons complained that they wanted lighter and healthier dishes. The original version was labor-intensive because you had to not only dice all the vegetables, but also blanch them in different pots. My version cuts out the blanching, and instead you roast the vegetables and end up with a sweet, caramelized, intensely flavored bite. Consider doubling the recipe; it only gets better the next day.

6 FIRST-COURSE SERVINGS

3 carrots, peeled

2 medium or 1 large zucchini

2 yellow summer squash

1 yellow bell pepper

1 red bell pepper

1 onion, thinly sliced

¼ cup olive oil

1 tablespoon dried Italian herbs or herbes de Provence

2 teaspoons kosher salt, plus more to taste

2 teaspoons freshly ground black pepper, plus more to taste

1 pound dried farfalle pasta (bow-tie pasta)

15 cherry tomatoes, halved

¾ cup shredded Parmesan cheese

PREHEAT THE OVEN to 450 degrees F. Cut the carrots, zucchini, squash, and bell peppers into thin 2-inch-long strips. On a large, heavy baking sheet, toss the vegetable strips, onion, oil, dried herbs, and 2 teaspoons each of salt and pepper to coat. Transfer half of the vegetable mixture to another large, heavy baking sheet, and arrange the vegetables evenly over both sheets. Bake, stirring after the first 10 minutes, until the carrots are tender and the other vegetables begin to brown, about 20 minutes total.

Meanwhile, bring a large pot of salted water to a boil. Add the farfalle and cook, stirring occasionally, until tender but still firm to the bite, about 8 minutes. Drain, reserving 1 cup of the cooking liquid. In a large bowl, toss the pasta with the cooked vegetables to combine. Add the cherry tomatoes and enough of the reserved cooking liquid to moisten. Season the pasta with more salt and pepper to taste.

Transfer the pasta to bowls. Sprinkle with Parmesan cheese and serve.

ZITI WITH ASPARAGUS,
Smoked Mozzarella, and Prosciutto

This is not merely everyday Italian, but Italian food in a flash. This dish would also work with penne, but definitely try to use one of these short tube shapes, which mimic the shape of the asparagus pieces and make for a beautiful presentation; with spaghetti, it's just not the same.

4 FIRST-COURSE SERVINGS

Salt

8 ounces dried ziti or other tubular pasta

1 pound asparagus, trimmed and cut diagonally into 1-inch pieces

2 tablespoons olive oil

2 garlic cloves, minced

½ teaspoon freshly ground black pepper, plus more to taste

3 ounces smoked mozzarella cheese, diced (about ½ cup)

3 ounces thinly sliced prosciutto, cut crosswise into strips

3 tablespoons thinly sliced fresh basil

BRING A LARGE POT of salted water to a boil. Add the ziti and cook for 5 minutes, stirring often. Add the asparagus and cook until the pasta is tender but still firm to the bite, and the asparagus is crisp-tender, about 2 minutes. Drain the pasta and asparagus, reserving 1 cup of the cooking liquid.

In a large, heavy skillet, heat the oil over a medium flame. Add the garlic and sauté until fragrant, about 20 seconds. Add the pasta, asparagus, ½ teaspoon each of salt and pepper, and the 1 cup of reserved cooking liquid, and toss to coat. Remove the skillet from the heat. Add the mozzarella, prosciutto, and basil and toss to combine. Season with more salt and pepper to taste. Transfer the pasta to shallow bowls and serve.

SPAGHETTI WITH CLAMS

Spaghetti with clams is very different from spaghetti with clam sauce. The former is a dish with a light, fragrant dressing tossed with whole clams; in my opinion, it's the only way to make this dish. It's also beautiful on the table; there's something about the shells combined with pasta that just looks so satisfying. And satisfying it is. You could also use mussels, for a twist, or small New Zealand cockles, whose refined shape and delicate flavor make for a more elegant version.

4 MAIN-COURSE SERVINGS

Salt	½ cup dry white wine
1 pound dried spaghetti	½ cup chopped fresh flat-leaf parsley
½ cup extra-virgin olive oil	½ teaspoon sea salt
2 shallots, finely chopped	½ teaspoon freshly ground black pepper
5 garlic cloves, finely chopped	2 tablespoons unsalted butter
2½ pounds Manila clams, scrubbed clean	Freshly grated zest of 1 lemon

BRING A LARGE POT of salted water to a boil. Add the spaghetti and cook until tender but still firm to the bite, stirring constantly in the beginning to prevent it from sticking together, about 8 minutes.

Meanwhile, in a large sauté pan, heat the oil over a medium-high flame. When almost smoking, add the shallots and sauté until soft, about 3 minutes. Add the garlic and sauté until the garlic is golden brown and the shallots are translucent, about 3 minutes (being careful not to burn the garlic). Add the clams, wine, 2 tablespoons of the parsley, and ½ teaspoon each of sea salt and pepper. Cover and simmer until most of the clams have opened, about 6 minutes (discard any shellfish that do not open). Whisk in the butter to thicken the sauce slightly.

Drain the spaghetti, reserving ⅓ cup of the cooking liquid. Do not rinse the spaghetti with water; you want to retain the natural starches that help the sauce adhere to the spaghetti. Toss the spaghetti with the clam mixture in the pan to coat. Add enough of the reserved cooking liquid to moisten.

Transfer the pasta to a large serving bowl. Sprinkle the lemon zest over the pasta. Garnish with the remaining parsley and serve immediately.

Everyday
INDULGENCES

I'm not going to kid you: These dishes aren't for dieters.

But richness has its place too, and nothing beats a per-

fectly cooked pasta dressed for elegance. So for that

special meal, try indulging yourself with these recipes.

PENNE À LA CARBONARA

There's only one thing I can say about this dish: It's so good you won't believe it.

4 MAIN-COURSE SERVINGS

2 tablespoons olive oil

1 pound pancetta, diced into 1-inch cubes

½ teaspoon freshly ground black pepper, plus more to taste

6 large eggs, at room temperature

½ cup heavy cream, at room temperature

1¼ cups freshly grated Parmesan cheese

½ teaspoon sea salt, plus more to taste

1 pound dried penne

2 tablespoons chopped fresh flat-leaf parsley

IN A LARGE SAUTÉ PAN, heat the oil over a medium flame. When almost smoking, add the pancetta and sauté until golden brown and crispy, about 5 minutes. Stir in ¼ teaspoon of black pepper and remove the pan from the heat.

In a medium bowl, beat the eggs and cream. Stir in ¼ cup of the Parmesan cheese, ½ teaspoon of sea salt, and ¼ teaspoon of pepper.

Meanwhile, bring a large pot of salted water to a boil. Add the penne and cook, stirring occasionally, until tender but still firm to the bite, about 8 minutes. Drain, reserving 1 cup of the cooking liquid. Do not rinse the pasta with water; you want to retain the pasta's natural starches that help the sauce adhere.

While the pasta is still hot, return it to the pot, and quickly toss with the browned pancetta, then the cream mixture. It's important to work quickly while the pasta is still hot so that the cream mixture will cook, but not curdle. Toss with the remaining cup of Parmesan cheese and the chopped parsley. Season the pasta with more salt and pepper to taste. Transfer the pasta to bowls and serve.

If you can't find **pancetta**, bacon is a good substitute.

FETTUCCINE ALFREDO

This famous cream sauce is named after its creator, Alfredo Di Lelio, who made it for his wife when she lost her appetite after the birth of their son. Alfredo's dish was made of egg-rich fettuccine, butter, and Parmigiano-Reggiano cheese, and it became a hit in his restaurant (Alfredo's) in Rome. In 1927, two Hollywood movie stars also fell in love with it and brought the recipe back to the States. The dish had to be adapted because the butter and Parmesan that were available here weren't as rich as they were in Italy. So chefs added heavy cream. I've added my own twist with the addition of lemon juice and zest. Fresh pasta is a must, because dried pasta can't stand up to all the rich ingredients.

6 FIRST-COURSE SERVINGS

1½ cups heavy cream

¼ cup fresh lemon juice (from about 1 lemon)

6 tablespoons unsalted butter

1 to 2 teaspoons grated lemon zest (from about 1 lemon)

   Pinch of freshly grated nutmeg

   Salt

9 ounces fresh fettuccine

1 cup freshly grated Parmesan cheese

¼ teaspoon freshly ground white pepper, plus more to taste

IN A LARGE, heavy skillet, stir 1 cup of the cream and the lemon juice to blend. Add the butter and cook over medium heat, stirring occasionally, just until the butter melts, about 3 minutes. Stir in the lemon zest and nutmeg. Remove from the heat.

Meanwhile, bring a large pot of salted water to a boil. Add the fettuccine and cook, stirring occasionally, until tender but still firm to the bite, about 4 minutes. Drain. Add the pasta, the remaining ½ cup of cream, the Parmesan, and ¼ teaspoon each of salt and pepper to the cream sauce in the skillet. Toss over low heat until the sauce thickens slightly, about 1 minute. Season with more salt and pepper to taste. Transfer the pasta to wide, shallow serving bowls and serve immediately.

BAKED RIGATONI
with Béchamel Sauce

Traditionally, this rich dish is served as a main course, and as a kid that's the way I ate it. But it also works in our health-conscious world as a starter or a side with something fresher and lighter—say, grilled fish drizzled with lemon juice or grilled meat. A creamy, cheesy dish like this is just the thing to make you feel coddled, as if your dining room is the coziest spot on earth.

6 SIDE-DISH SERVINGS

1 teaspoon olive oil

4 cups Béchamel Sauce (page 79)

½ pound thinly sliced prosciutto, cut crosswise into thin strips

1 cup freshly grated fontina cheese

½ teaspoon salt, plus more to taste

Pinch of freshly ground white pepper, plus more to taste

1 pound dried rigatoni

3 tablespoons unsalted butter, diced

PREHEAT THE OVEN to 425 degrees F. Lightly coat a 13 × 9-inch glass baking dish with the oil. In a medium saucepan, stir the béchamel sauce over medium heat until hot (do not allow the sauce to boil). Stir in the prosciutto, ½ cup of the fontina cheese, ½ teaspoon of salt, and a pinch of white pepper. Set the cheese sauce aside.

Bring a large pot of salted water to a boil. Add the rigatoni and cook, stirring occasionally, until almost tender but still very firm, about 5 minutes (do not cook the pasta to doneness at this point, since it will continue cooking as it bakes in the oven). Drain the pasta and return it to the pot. Stir in the cheese sauce and season the pasta mixture with more salt and pepper to taste.

Spoon the pasta mixture into the prepared dish, then sprinkle with the remaining ½ cup of fontina cheese and dot the top with the butter. (The pasta can be prepared up to this point 8 hours ahead. Cover and refrigerate. Uncover before baking.) Bake the pasta until the top is golden brown and the sauce bubbles, about 25 minutes. Serve immediately.

Leftover
PASTA

We've all been there: Without thinking, you just dump that whole pound of pasta into the boiling water. Once it's plumped up and drained, you realize that it's far more pasta than your appetite can handle. Don't despair—and don't throw it away. Take a hint from the Italians, who are incredibly inventive when it comes to leftovers, and try the following recipes.

PIZZA DI SPAGHETTI

Like a pizza, it's crunchy on the outside and tender on the inside. Nearly any pasta shape with any sauce will do; as long as you liked the original serving, you'll like the leftovers prepared this way.

4 SIDE-DISH SERVINGS

1 cup freshly grated Parmesan cheese, plus extra for garnish

½ cup whole milk

2 large eggs

½ teaspoon sea salt

½ teaspoon freshly ground black pepper

2 cups leftover cooked and sauced pasta, such as spaghetti with Tomato Sauce with Olives (page 60)

½ cup olive oil

IN A LARGE BOWL, beat the 1 cup of Parmesan cheese, the milk, eggs, sea salt, and pepper. Add the leftover pasta and toss to coat.

In a 10-inch-diameter nonstick sauté pan, heat the oil over a medium flame. Add the pasta mixture to the pan, spreading evenly. Cook until golden brown on the bottom, about 8 minutes. Carefully invert the pasta mixture onto a plate, then slide it back into the pan. Continue cooking until the bottom is golden brown and the mixture is heated through, about 6 minutes. Transfer the pasta mixture to a serving platter and sprinkle with Parmesan cheese. Cut into wedges and serve warm.

TORTA DI PASTA

The literal translation of torta di pasta *is "cake made of pasta." What I particularly love about this recipe is that it makes for great finger food: All the ingredients bind together and can be cut up into easy little servings, and it can be served at room temperature. You probably won't want to tell your guests that you're serving them leftovers, and they'll never know the difference.*

6 APPETIZER SERVINGS OR 4 MAIN-COURSE SERVINGS

Salt

8 ounces dried spaghetti, or leftover cooked pasta

½ cup drained oil-packed sun-dried tomatoes, chopped

4 large eggs

¾ cup freshly grated Parmesan cheese

¾ cup freshly grated fontina cheese

1½ teaspoons salt

½ teaspoon freshly ground black pepper

1 tablespoon unsalted butter

1 tablespoon olive oil

IF USING DRIED PASTA, bring a large pot of salted water to a boil. Add the spaghetti and cook, stirring occasionally, until tender but still firm to the bite, about 8 minutes. Drain. In a large bowl, toss the spaghetti with the sun-dried tomatoes, then set aside to cool.

In a medium bowl, whisk the eggs, Parmesan cheese, fontina cheese, 1½ teaspoons of salt, and the pepper to blend. Add the egg mixture to the cooled spaghetti mixture, and toss to coat.

Preheat the broiler. In a 9½-inch-diameter ovenproof nonstick skillet, melt the butter and oil over medium heat. Transfer the spaghetti mixture to the skillet, pressing to form an even layer. Cook until the bottom is golden brown, about 3 minutes. Transfer the skillet to the oven and broil until the top is golden brown, about 5 minutes. Let the torta cool in the skillet to room temperature, then invert it onto a platter. Cut the torta into wedges and serve at room temperature.

Everyday

POLENTA

Polenta is cornmeal (dried ground corn) cooked in a liquid until it swells. It's Italy's version of mashed potatoes. A piping hot bowl is excellent served with meats or stews, or polenta can be fried into sticks and dipped in marinara sauce, or baked and topped with all sorts of sauces; there are so many great ways to serve it. Polenta is easy to make, but the traditional cooking method takes some muscle because you need to stir constantly for 30 to 40 minutes. In order to save time, I often use instant polenta, which is partially cooked, meaning half the work is already done for you.

BASIC POLENTA

This is the most basic, fundamental version of polenta. It's the perfect side to accompany a delicious, long-simmered stew. Or you can serve this basic recipe topped with your favorite sauce; I'm partial to bolognese.

6 SIDE-DISH SERVINGS

6 cups water

2 teaspoons salt

1¾ cups yellow cornmeal

3 tablespoons unsalted butter, cut into pieces

IN A LARGE, heavy saucepan, bring the water to a boil. Add the salt, then gradually whisk in the cornmeal. Reduce the heat to low and cook, stirring often, until the mixture thickens and the cornmeal is tender, about 15 minutes. Remove from the heat and stir in the butter.

Transfer the polenta to a bowl and serve.

FRIED POLENTA

Better than French fries—and a great snack or appetizer. You can use other dipping sauces, but the simplicity of a good marinara is hard to beat here.

MAKES 30 PIECES

1 teaspoon plus ½ cup olive oil

3 cups Basic Polenta (page 121), freshly made and hot

¼ cup freshly grated Parmesan cheese

2 teaspoons salt

1 cup Marinara Sauce (page 59)

COAT AN 11 X 7-INCH baking dish with 1 teaspoon of oil. Transfer the hot polenta to the prepared baking dish, spreading evenly to ¾ inch thick. Cover and refrigerate until cold and firm, about 2 hours.

Preheat the oven to 250 degrees F. Cut the polenta into 2 × 1-inch pieces. In a large, heavy skillet, heat the remaining ½ cup of oil over a medium-high flame. Working in batches, fry the polenta pieces until golden brown on all sides, about 3 minutes per side. Using tongs, transfer the polenta pieces to paper towels and drain. Place the polenta pieces on a baking sheet and keep warm in the oven while cooking the remaining batches.

Transfer the polenta pieces to a serving platter. Sprinkle the polenta with the Parmesan cheese and salt, and serve, passing the marinara sauce alongside.

When I make **polenta** I like to use a heavy-bottomed saucepan

because it cooks the polenta evenly and helps develop rich, creamy, sweet corn flavor.

BAKED POLENTA

I'm using instant polenta for this recipe because it works so well for my polenta party: I invite six friends over, and I cut the baked polenta into triangles and serve it with three different sauces: Simple Bolognese (page 65), Spicy Tomato Sauce (page 62), and Mushroom Ragù (page 80). My guests top the triangles with their choice of sauces, and there you have it: a new and easy way to entertain.

6 SIDE-DISH SERVINGS OR 4 MAIN-COURSE SERVINGS

2 teaspoons vegetable oil

6 cups cold water

1 teaspoon sea salt

1 teaspoon freshly ground black pepper

1 (13-ounce) package instant polenta

PREHEAT THE OVEN to 350 degrees F. Lightly oil an 11 × 7-inch baking sheet, then line the baking sheet with wax paper.

In a large pot, combine the water, sea salt, and pepper, and bring to a boil. Reduce the heat to medium-high and slowly stir in the polenta. Continue stirring the polenta until it is thick and smooth, about 5 minutes. Pour the polenta onto the lined baking sheet, and bake in the oven until the polenta is slightly firm to the touch, about 15 minutes. Remove from the oven and let cool slightly. When the polenta is cool enough to handle, cut it into desired shapes, such as triangles, squares, diamonds, or rounds.

CREAMY POLENTA
with Gorgonzola Cheese

As an alternative to mashed potatoes, try making this mouthwatering polenta. Nearly any easily melted cheese will do, but I happen to love the taste of the king of Italian blue cheese, Gorgonzola. It's available in either sweet (dolce) or more tangy (piccante) versions, and the choice is really up to you. If you have access to a good cheese counter, they'll let you taste before you buy. And if Gorgonzola isn't available but you still want to make this dish—and trust me, you really do—you can use any good blue cheese, such as Roquefort, Stilton, or Bleu d'Auvergne.

6 SIDE-DISH SERVINGS

¾ cup heavy cream

3 ounces Gorgonzola cheese, cut into pieces

¼ teaspoon salt, plus more to taste

¼ teaspoon freshly ground black pepper, plus more to taste
   Basic Polenta (page 121), freshly made and hot

ADD THE CREAM, Gorgonzola, and ¼ teaspoon each of salt and pepper to the freshly made polenta while it is still in the saucepan, and stir until the cheese melts. Season the polenta with more salt and pepper to taste. Transfer the polenta to a bowl and serve.

Everyday
RISOTTO

When we think of Italian cuisine, the first starch that comes to mind is pasta. But in Italy, risotto is just as popular. Like pasta, it's something of a neutral canvas and can be flavored in many different ways. The key to a good risotto is the rice. Arborio, a short-grain variety, is my choice for a creamy, velvety risotto. ∎ Another key to a successful risotto is the gradual addition of the cooking liquid. Unlike many rice dishes, for risotto you don't combine a set amount of rice with a set amount of liquid and cook it all together. With risotto, you add the liquid in small increments, stirring all the while and allowing the rice to absorb the liquid, for about 20 minutes. So risotto isn't the thing to serve if your other dishes involve last-minute preparations; you don't want to be stirring the risotto with one hand while trying to sauté chicken breasts with the other. For that reason, I like to serve risotto with something that comes out of the oven: a slow-braised stew, for example, or any roast.

BASIC RISOTTO

This is the most basic risotto. But just because it's basic doesn't mean it's not great: This dish is all about the crunchy yet creamy rice combined with the nuttiness of Parmesan. I serve this basic version as a side to main dishes that have strong, flavored sauces, using the simplicity of the rice to offset the complexity of the entrée.

6 SIDE-DISH SERVINGS

4   cups reduced-sodium chicken broth

3   tablespoons butter

¾   cup finely chopped onion (from 1 onion)

1½ cups Arborio rice or medium-grain white rice

½   cup dry white wine

½   cup freshly grated Parmesan cheese

½   teaspoon salt

¼   teaspoon freshly ground black pepper

IN A MEDIUM SAUCEPAN, bring the broth to a simmer. Cover the broth and keep hot over low heat.

In a large, heavy saucepan, melt 2 tablespoons of the butter over medium heat. Add the onion and sauté until tender but not brown, about 3 minutes. Add the rice and stir to coat with the butter. Add the wine and simmer until the wine has almost completely evaporated, about 3 minutes. Add ½ cup of simmering broth and stir until almost completely absorbed, about 2 minutes. Continue cooking the rice, adding the broth ½ cup at a time, stirring constantly and allowing each addition of broth to absorb before adding the next, until the rice is tender but still firm to the bite and the mixture is creamy, about 20 minutes total. Remove from the heat. Stir in the Parmesan cheese, the remaining tablespoon of butter, and the salt and pepper. Transfer the risotto to a serving bowl and serve immediately.

You can add *just about anything you want to basic risotto: prosciutto, vegetables such as peas, seafood such as shrimp, or herbs and other seasonings such as saffron. (The recipe that follows is for one of my favorite variations of the basic risotto, with wild mushrooms and peas.) But you usually don't want these ingredients to cook for 30 minutes with the rice, or they'd become overcooked—tough, dry, and flavorless. So instead of cooking these other ingredients with your rice, cook them separately.*

To save dirtying another pan, you can cook the other ingredients before you start with the basic risotto recipe, in the same pan that you'll use for the rice. On the other hand, to save time, you can use another pan, and cook them while you're making the risotto.

WILD MUSHROOM RISOTTO
with Peas

The secret to the intense mushroom flavor in this recipe is that not only are mush-rooms themselves part of the mix, but the risotto is cooked with mushroom-flavored broth. In order to use dried porcini mushrooms—or any dried mushrooms for that matter—you have to reconstitute them by allowing them to sit in hot water for a few minutes, absorbing that water and plumping up. Then the mushrooms are ready to cook with, and you have all this flavorful liquid as a by-product. By all means, take advantage of it: Here, it works as a flavor booster to the chicken stock; but you can also use it as the base of a wonderful soup or sauce.

6 SIDE-DISH SERVINGS

5¾ cups canned low-sodium chicken broth

½ ounce dried porcini mushrooms

¼ cup (½ stick) unsalted butter

2 cups finely chopped onion

10 ounces white mushrooms, finely chopped

2 garlic cloves, minced

1½ cups Arborio rice or medium-grain white rice

⅔ cup dry white wine

½ cup frozen peas, thawed

⅔ cup freshly grated Parmesan cheese

Salt and freshly ground black pepper

BRING THE BROTH to a simmer in a heavy, medium-size saucepan. Add the porcini mushrooms. Cover and set aside until the mushrooms are tender, about 5 minutes. Using a slotted spoon, remove the mushrooms and finely chop. Cover the broth and keep warm over very low heat.

Melt the butter in a large, heavy saucepan over medium heat. Add the onions and sauté until tender, about 8 minutes. Add the white mush-rooms, porcini mushrooms, and garlic; sauté until the mushrooms are tender and the juices evaporate, about 10 minutes. Stir in the rice. Add the wine; cook, stirring often, until the liquid is absorbed, about 2 minutes. Add 1 cup of hot broth; simmer over medium-low heat, stirring often, until the liquid is absorbed, about 3 minutes. Continue to cook until the rice is just tender and the mixture is creamy, adding more broth by cupfuls and stirring often, about 28 minutes. Stir in the peas. Mix in the Parmesan cheese. Season with salt and pepper to taste.

RISOTTO AL SALTO
(Rice Cake)

Another fantastic use for leftover risotto, and a great afternoon snack.

4 APPETIZER SERVINGS

2 cups Wild Mushroom Risotto with Peas (page 131), cold

¼ cup plus 2 tablespoons freshly grated Parmesan cheese

1 tablespoon unsalted butter

1 tablespoon olive oil

IN A MEDIUM BOWL, stir the risotto and ¼ cup of the Parmesan cheese to blend. In a heavy, large skillet, melt the butter and oil over medium-low heat. Add the risotto to the skillet and press into a 7-inch-diameter disc. Sprinkle the remaining 2 tablespoons of Parmesan cheese over the risotto cake. Cover and cook for 10 minutes, then uncover and continue to cook until the risotto cake is golden brown on the bottom and set around the edges, about 5 minutes longer. Using a large metal spatula, loosen the risotto cake from the pan and slide it onto a plate. Cut the risotto cake into wedges and serve.

ARANCINI DI RISO

Arancini di Riso *means "little orange rice balls"—orange, because the risotto was traditionally made with saffron (the version called Risotto Milanese), which gives the rice an orange tint. This recipe is one of the many brilliant ways that Italians have for using up leftovers.*

MAKES ABOUT 20

2 cups Basic Risotto (page 128), cooled

1½ cups dried Italian-style bread crumbs

½ cup freshly grated Parmesan cheese

2 large eggs, beaten to blend

2 ounces mozzarella cheese, cut into ½-inch cubes

Vegetable oil (for deep-frying)

IN A LARGE BOWL, stir the risotto, ½ cup of the bread crumbs, the Parmesan cheese, and the eggs to combine. In a medium bowl, place the remaining cup of bread crumbs. Using about 2 tablespoons of the risotto mixture for each cube of mozzarella cheese, form the risotto mixture around the cheese cubes to enclose completely and form into 1¾-inch-diameter balls. Roll the balls in the remaining bread crumbs to coat.

In a large, heavy saucepan, add enough oil to reach a depth of 3 inches and heat over a medium flame to 350 degrees F. Working in batches, add the rice balls and cook until brown and heated through, about 4 minutes. Using a slotted spoon, transfer the rice balls to paper towels to drain. Let rest for 2 minutes. Serve hot.

everyday

entreés

EVERYDAY GRILLS AND SAUTÉS

Grilled Jumbo Shrimp ▪ Scampi on Couscous ▪ Grilled Seafood Salad ▪ Grilled Tuna Steaks ▪ Seared Rib-Eye Steak with Arugula–Roasted Pepper Salad ▪ Steak Florentine ▪ Grilled Lamb Chops

EVERYDAY CUTLETS

Chicken Parmesan ▪ Chicken Piccata ▪ Chicken Saltimbocca ▪ Veal Marsala ▪ Pork Milanese ▪ Braciola

EVERYDAY ROASTS

Roasted Red Snapper with Rosemary ▪ Salmon Baked in Foil ▪ Roasted Pork Loin with Fig Sauce ▪ Roasted Chicken with Balsamic Vinaigrette ▪ Turkey Tonnato ▪ Aunt Raffy's Turkey Stuffing

EVERYDAY STEWS AND SAUCES

Chicken Spezzatino ▪ Chicken Cacciatore ▪ Shrimp Fra Diavolo ▪ Mussels, Clams, and Shrimp in Spicy Tomato Broth ▪ Easy Osso Buco

EVERYDAY LEFTOVERS

Steak Salad ▪ Milanese Sandwich ▪ Grilled-Seafood Risotto

Everyday
GRILLS AND SAUTÉS

Brushed with a little olive oil, sprinkled with some herbs, finished with a squeeze of lemon juice—the classic Italian preparations of meat, fish, and poultry simply rely on the natural flavors of good ingredients, to which the cook does as little as possible. ■ The key to all of these recipes is high heat; your grill, your pan, your oil should all be hot. Whether you're grilling to create a charred crust or sautéing to lightly brown, you want it to happen quickly. Give your cooking surfaces plenty of time to warm up, always bring your oil up to high heat before adding the food, and make sure that your food has plenty of room in your pans; an overcrowded skillet is definitely not what you're looking for. ■ And of course the beauty of all of these is the cooking speed: We're talking mere minutes over the flame, whether it's shrimp or steak. This food is quick, easy, and supremely satisfying.

Grilled
JUMBO SHRIMP

While a lexicographer might say that "jumbo shrimp" is an oxymoron, a chef knows it means something specific: Shrimp are marketed according to size, with different classifications depending on how many shrimp will constitute a pound. Jumbo shrimp are 11 to 15 per pound, and extra-large are 16 to 20 per pound; at the other end of the scale, miniature are 100 per pound, and small are 36 to 45. In general, the larger the shrimp, the more expensive they are; but if you're peeling them or handling them in any way, the larger they are, the less work you have to do. A trade-off, like many things.

4 APPETIZER SERVINGS OR 2 MAIN-COURSE SERVINGS

1   teaspoon plus 2 tablespoons olive oil

1   pound jumbo shrimp

2   tablespoons salt

BRUSH 1 TEASPOON of oil over a barbecue rack or a ridged grill pan. Prepare a charcoal or gas grill for high heat or preheat the grill pan over a high flame. Using scissors, cut the shell down the center of the back of the shrimp. Brush the shrimp with the remaining 2 tablespoons of oil and sprinkle with salt. Grill the shrimp until just cooked through, about 3 minutes per side. Transfer the shrimp to a plate and serve.

Serve with
spaghetti with Arugula Pesto
(PAGE 77)

SCAMPI ON COUSCOUS

It may seem strange to have a dish using couscous (made of semolina flour) in an Italian cookbook, but couscous is actually a staple of Sicilian cooking. Over the centuries, southern Italian—and especially Sicilian—culture has been greatly influenced by North Africa and Greece, and this recipe is a perfect culinary example.

4 MAIN-COURSE SERVINGS

½ cup plus 1 tablespoon extra-virgin olive oil

1 small onion, chopped

1 carrot, peeled and chopped

3 garlic cloves, minced

2 (8-ounce) cans chopped tomatoes in their juice

1 (8-ounce) bottle clam juice

¼ cup dry white wine

1 teaspoon salt, plus more to taste

¼ teaspoon freshly ground black pepper, plus more to taste

About 1¼ cups water

2 cups plain couscous

2 pounds large shrimp, peeled and deveined

Juice of 1 lemon

1 tablespoon chopped fresh flat-leaf parsley

1 teaspoon dried crushed red pepper flakes

IN A LARGE POT, heat ¼ cup of the oil over a medium-high flame. When almost smoking, add the onion, carrot, and half of the garlic and sauté until the onion is soft, about 5 minutes. Add the tomatoes with their juice, clam juice, wine, ½ teaspoon of salt, and ¼ teaspoon of black pepper. Bring to a boil and simmer uncovered over medium heat until the liquid reduces and the tomatoes break down, about 10 minutes. Remove from the heat and let cool slightly. Carefully transfer the tomato mixture to the bowl of a food processor and purée until smooth, adding water a couple of tablespoons at a time to form a broth consistency. (The tomato broth can be made 1 day ahead. Cool, then cover and refrigerate. Bring the tomato broth to a simmer before continuing.)

In a medium saucepan, combine 2 cups of the tomato broth, 1 cup of water, and 1 tablespoon of oil. Bring the mixture to a boil, then stir in the couscous. Remove from the heat. Cover and set aside until the couscous has absorbed the liquid, about 10 minutes. Season the couscous with more salt and pepper to taste. Keep the remaining tomato broth warm.

In a large skillet, heat the remaining ¼ cup of oil over a medium flame. Add the remaining garlic and sauté until fragrant, about 20 seconds. Add the shrimp and sauté until the shrimp just begin to turn pink, about 5 minutes (be careful not to overcook the shrimp or they will become tough). Remove from the heat and stir in the lemon juice, parsley, red pepper flakes, and the remaining ½ teaspoon of salt.

Spoon the couscous into the center of serving plates and top with the shrimp. Spoon some of the remaining tomato broth around the couscous and serve.

GRILLED SEAFOOD SALAD

This is a beautiful dish, which I discovered on vacation with my family in Capri. Every year, we visit the same hotel—Hotel Quisisana—on this beautiful island in southern Italy. The region is rich in seafood, which they use for everything from antipasti to entrées. Some of the seafood can be a bit exotic for most American palates, especially squid. But don't be afraid of it: You can buy squid that's already cleaned from your fishmonger, and all you need to do is rinse, grill, and slice. Just like chicken. (Okay, not really just like chicken, but the steps are the same.)

4 MAIN-COURSE SERVINGS

½ cup olive oil

2 garlic cloves, finely chopped

1 tablespoon chopped fresh flat-leaf parsley

1 teaspoon chopped fresh marjoram

1 teaspoon chopped fresh thyme

¼ cup fresh lemon juice (from about 1 lemon)

1 teaspoon salt, plus more to taste

1 teaspoon freshly ground black pepper, plus more to taste

12 ounces sea scallops

12 ounces cleaned squid, bodies only

1 (15-ounce) can white cannellini beans, drained and rinsed

3 ounces arugula leaves (about 6 cups)

2 carrots, peeled and cut into thin strips (approximately 2 inches long)

½ yellow bell pepper, cut into thin strips (approximately 2 inches long)

1 large head of radicchio, leaves separated

IN A SMALL, heavy skillet, heat the oil over a medium flame. Add the garlic and herbs, and sauté until fragrant, about 30 seconds. Cool to room temperature, then whisk in the lemon juice and ½ teaspoon each of salt and pepper. Set the dressing aside.

Prepare a charcoal or gas grill for medium-high heat or preheat a ridged grill pan over a medium-high flame. Pat the scallops and squid dry with

(recipe continues)

paper towels, then brush them with 2 tablespoons of the dressing and sprinkle with ½ teaspoon each of salt and pepper. Thread the scallops onto skewers and grill the scallops and squid until just cooked through, turning once, about 2 minutes per side. Cool completely. Remove the scallops from the skewers and cut the squid crosswise into ¼-inch-wide rings.

In a large bowl, combine the beans, arugula, carrots, and bell pepper. Toss with enough dressing to coat. Season with more salt and pepper to taste.

Place 1 large or 2 medium radicchio leaves on each of 4 plates. Spoon the bean salad into the radicchio cups, and top with the scallops and squid. Drizzle the remaining dressing over and serve.

GRILLED TUNA STEAKS

Besides their wonderful flavor, one of the things that's remarkable about tuna steaks is simply how great they look, especially with grill marks on the outside and a nice brown crust concealing a tender, still-red interior. And tuna steaks really hold their shape after grilling; no falling-apart flakiness here. To achieve those beautiful grill marks, you need to leave the steaks alone for a couple minutes; don't turn or move them, at all. Resist the temptation to tamper, and just let them alone. And to get that perfectly seared outside while maintaining a nice rare (or even raw, if that's your preference) interior, just pop your steaks in the freezer for an hour before you grill.

4 MAIN-COURSE SERVINGS

2 ahi tuna steaks (each about 1 pound and 2 inches thick)

¼ cup extra-virgin olive oil

¾ teaspoon kosher salt

¾ teaspoon freshly ground black pepper

2 tablespoons fresh lemon juice (from about ½ lemon)

   Basil Pesto (page 72)

PREPARE A CHARCOAL or gas grill for medium-high heat or preheat a ridged grill pan over a medium-high flame. Wash and pat the tuna dry with paper towels. Brush both sides of the tuna with the oil and sprinkle with the salt and pepper. Grill the tuna until just seared on the outside but still rare in the center, about 2 minutes per side. If desired, continue cooking the tuna until just cooked through in the center, about 2 minutes longer per side. Using a metal spatula, transfer the tuna to a cutting board and set aside for 5 minutes.

Using a large, sharp knife, cut the tuna across the grain and on a bias into ½-inch-thick slices. Arrange the slices on a serving plate. Drizzle with the lemon juice, and serve with the basil pesto.

SEARED RIB-EYE STEAK
with Arugula–Roasted Pepper Salad

I love the way the hot steak wilts the arugula, and how the meat's juices mingle with the dressing. You could make this with any steak (or, for that matter, chicken or pork), but rib eye is the classic choice. Whichever cut, it's vitally important to let the cooked meat rest before carving, so the juices redistribute and settle, keeping your meat moist and tender.

4 MAIN-COURSE SERVINGS

- 7 tablespoons extra-virgin olive oil
- 2 rib-eye steaks (about 1 pound each and 1 inch thick)
- 1½ teaspoons kosher salt, plus more to taste
- 1½ teaspoons freshly ground black pepper, plus more to taste
- 3 cups fresh arugula, washed and spun dry
- 1½ cups sliced roasted red bell peppers (page 51), rinsed and patted dry
- 2 tablespoons balsamic vinegar
- 1 small block of Parmesan cheese (about 8 ounces)

RUB 2 TABLESPOONS of the oil over the steaks, then sprinkle with 1 teaspoon each of salt and pepper. In a large sauté pan, heat 1 tablespoon of the oil over a medium-high flame. Add the steaks and fry until seared on the outside and cooked to desired doneness, about 5 minutes per side for medium-rare (in order to help create a good, crusty sear, do not move or pierce the meat as it cooks on each side). Using tongs, transfer the steaks to a large plate and let rest for 10 minutes.

Line a large platter with the arugula. Tear the roasted peppers into large pieces and scatter over the arugula. In a small bowl, whisk the remaining 4 tablespoons of oil, the balsamic vinegar, ½ teaspoon each of salt and pepper, and any juices from the steaks that have accumulated on the plate. Season the dressing with more salt and pepper to taste.

Cut the steaks across the grain and diagonally into 1½-inch-thick slices. Lay the slices atop the arugula and peppers, and drizzle with the dressing. Using a vegetable peeler, shave the Parmesan cheese over and serve immediately.

STEAK FLORENTINE

This famous T-bone recipe from Florence is the perfect steak: The outside of the meat caramelizes when it hits the hot grill, and the light garlic aroma and final drizzle of olive oil provide just the flavor elements to make a great piece of meat into a fantastic entrée.

4 TO 6 MAIN-COURSE SERVINGS

1   large garlic clove, halved

2   T-bone steaks (each about 1½ pounds, and 1¼ to 1½ inches thick)

1½ teaspoons kosher salt

1½ teaspoons freshly ground black pepper

½   lemon, halved

2   teaspoons olive oil

PREPARE A CHARCOAL or gas grill for medium heat or preheat a ridged grill pan over a medium flame. Rub the garlic clove over the meat and the bone of the steaks and sprinkle the steaks with the salt and pepper. Grill the steaks until cooked to desired doneness, turning once, about 5 minutes per side for rare, and 7 minutes per side for medium-rare. Transfer the steaks to a cutting board and squeeze the lemon over the steaks. Drizzle with the oil. Let the steaks rest for 5 minutes before serving.

GRILLED LAMB CHOPS

Easter is a real family holiday for Italians, and lamb was our usual fare for Easter supper—usually a leg or a crown roast. When it's not Easter supper, though, I usually go for the smaller portions and simplicity of separate chops, as in this recipe. Rosemary and garlic are the perfect companions to lamb, and the paste below is a wonderful way to season the meat with a minimum of effort. This combo also works superbly with any cut of lamb; just double the quantities for a full rack, or triple them for a leg.

2 MAIN-COURSE SERVINGS

2   tablespoons extra-virgin olive oil

2   large garlic cloves

1   tablespoon fresh rosemary leaves, coarsely chopped

1   teaspoon fresh thyme leaves

½   teaspoon sea salt

    Pinch of cayenne pepper

6   lamb chops (each about ¾ inch thick)

IN A FOOD PROCESSOR fitted with a metal blade, blend the oil, garlic, rosemary, thyme, sea salt, and cayenne pepper to form a paste. Rub the paste over the lamb chops and marinate for at least 30 minutes and up to 4 hours.

Heat a grill pan over a high flame until almost smoking. Add the chops and sear for 2 minutes on each side. Reduce the heat to medium and cook the lamb chops to desired doneness, about 3 minutes longer per side for medium-rare. Transfer the lamb chops to two plates, dividing equally, and serve. •

Everyday
CUTLETS

I use the word *cutlet* for any thin, boneless, skinless piece of veal, pork, or chicken. For veal, your butcher will have "cutlet" meat; for pork, I usually use a boneless chop, pounded thin; and for chicken, a boneless, skinless breast, sliced crosswise and pounded thin. ∎ These are perhaps the ultimate in *Everyday Italian* entrée choices: They cook *extremely* quickly, and you can top them with just about anything you like. And the meats are pretty interchangeable in many recipes; you can mix and match the meat from one recipe with the sauce or preparation from another. (You've probably noticed this on menus—Chicken Marsala and Veal Marsala, Chicken Parmigiana and Veal Parmigiana. The restaurants mix and match, and so can you.) Just remember that cooking times vary, and it's especially important not to overcook veal (or it becomes tough and loses its delicate flavor) or undercook chicken or pork (for safety's sake). Other than that, though, go forth into the world of cutlets—the ultimate in flexibility, ease, and speed, not to mention a great variety of classic Italian dishes and some new favorites.

CHICKEN PARMESAN

Perhaps the all-time number-one most popular Italian-American dish, Chicken Parmesan is often made of thickly breaded chicken cutlets topped with way too much cheese and garlicky tomato sauce. (And in many restaurants, if you can locate the actual Parmesan in the "Chicken Parmesan," you should win a huge prize.) I wanted to remain true to the heartiness of the dish, but I also wanted to lighten it up a bit. So I don't bread my cutlets, but instead brown them in a skillet before adding the topping and baking them.

4 MAIN-COURSE SERVINGS

1 tablespoon olive oil

1 teaspoon chopped fresh thyme

1 teaspoon chopped fresh rosemary

1 teaspoon chopped fresh flat-leaf parsley

4 chicken cutlets (about 3 ounces each)

1 teaspoon salt

½ teaspoon freshly ground black pepper

¾ cup Marinara Sauce (page 59)

¼ cup shredded mozzarella cheese

8 teaspoons freshly grated Parmesan cheese

1 tablespoon unsalted butter, cut into pieces

PREHEAT THE OVEN to 500 degrees F. In a small bowl, stir the oil and herbs to blend. Brush both sides of the cutlets with the herb oil and sprinkle with the salt and pepper. Heat a large, heavy ovenproof skillet over a high flame. Add the cutlets and cook just until brown, about 1 minute per side. Remove from the heat.

Spoon the marinara sauce over and around the cutlets. Sprinkle 1 tablespoon of mozzarella over each cutlet, then sprinkle 2 teaspoons of Parmesan over each. Dot the tops with the butter pieces, and bake until the cheese melts and the chicken is cooked through, about 5 minutes.

CHICKEN PICCATA

This is the lightest of the cutlet recipes, with the bright, acidic lemon juice perfectly complemented by the briny capers and the fresh parsley. Be sure to keep your dusting of flour light; you're not making a thick egg-and-bread-crumb coating.

4 MAIN-COURSE SERVINGS

4 skinless, boneless chicken breasts, halved crosswise

½ teaspoon sea salt

½ teaspoon freshly ground black pepper

   All-purpose flour, for dredging

4 tablespoons unsalted butter

2 tablespoons extra-virgin olive oil

½ cup reduced-sodium chicken broth

⅓ cup fresh lemon juice (from about 2 lemons)

¼ cup drained capers, rinsed

2 tablespoons chopped fresh flat-leaf parsley

SPRINKLE THE CHICKEN with the salt and pepper. Dredge the chicken in the flour to coat lightly. In a large sauté pan, melt 2 tablespoons of the butter with the 2 tablespoons of oil over medium-high heat. Add the chicken and cook just until brown, about 3 minutes per side. Using tongs, transfer the chicken to a plate.

Add the broth, lemon juice, and capers to the same pan. Bring the broth mixture to a boil over medium-high heat, scraping up the brown bits from the bottom of the pan for extra flavor. Return the chicken to the pan and simmer until just cooked through, about 5 minutes. Using tongs, transfer the chicken to a platter. Whisk the remaining 2 tablespoons of butter into the sauce. Pour the sauce over the chicken, garnish with the parsley, and serve.

CHICKEN SALTIMBOCCA

Saltimbocca *means "leap in the mouth"*—as in, this traditional Roman dish is so good that surprisingly it will just leap into your mouth. In Italy they make this dish with veal, but I find that the delicate flavors of veal get lost amid the strong tastes of the spinach and prosciutto, and I end up feeling like the very expensive veal cutlets were a waste of money. So I use chicken.

6 MAIN-COURSE SERVINGS

1 (10-ounce) box frozen chopped spinach, thawed

3 tablespoons olive oil

1¼ teaspoons salt, plus more to taste

1 teaspoon freshly ground black pepper, plus more to taste

6 chicken cutlets (3 ounces each), pounded to flatten evenly

6 paper-thin slices of prosciutto

¼ cup freshly shredded Parmesan cheese

1 (14-ounce) can reduced-sodium chicken broth

3 tablespoons fresh lemon juice (from 1 lemon)

SQUEEZE THE FROZEN SPINACH to remove the excess water. In a small bowl, toss the spinach with 1 tablespoon of the oil to coat. Season with ¼ teaspoon each of salt and pepper.

Place the chicken cutlets flat on a work surface. Sprinkle with 1 teaspoon of salt and ¾ teaspoon of pepper. Lay 1 slice of prosciutto atop each chicken cutlet. Arrange an even layer of spinach atop the prosciutto and sprinkle the Parmesan cheese evenly over each. Beginning at the short tapered end, roll up each cutlet as for a jelly roll and secure with a toothpick.

In a large, heavy skillet, heat the remaining 2 tablespoons of oil over a high flame. Add the chicken rolls and cook just until golden brown, about 2 minutes per side. Add the broth and lemon juice and bring to a boil. Reduce the heat to medium, cover, and simmer until the chicken is just cooked through, about 4 minutes.

Using tongs, transfer the chicken to 6 plates and set aside. Increase the heat to high and cook the sauce until it is reduced to about ⅔ cup, about 5 minutes. Season with salt and pepper to taste. Drizzle the sauce over the chicken, and serve.

VEAL MARSALA

This classic Italian-American dish is a prime example of a versatile preparation—you'll find Marsala recipes made with veal, pork, chicken, and even steak. Not surprisingly, the key is the Marsala wine, which for centuries has been one of the prized treasures of Sicily. It's a fortified wine—like Portugal's port or Spain's sherry—and can be either sweet, which is the type used for cooking, or dry.

4 MAIN-COURSE SERVINGS

8 veal cutlets (about 3 ounces each)

1¼ teaspoons salt, plus more to taste

1 teaspoon freshly ground black pepper, plus more to taste

4 tablespoons unsalted butter

2 tablespoons olive oil

1 large shallot, finely chopped

2 garlic cloves, minced

4 ounces assorted mushrooms, sliced

½ cup sweet Marsala

1 sprig of fresh rosemary

¾ cup reduced-sodium chicken broth

SPRINKLE THE VEAL with ¾ teaspoon each of salt and pepper. In a large, heavy skillet, melt 1 tablespoon of the butter and 1 tablespoon of the oil over medium-high heat. Add 4 of the veal cutlets and cook until golden brown, about 1½ minutes per side. Using tongs, transfer the veal to a plate. Add another tablespoon of butter and tablespoon of oil to the skillet and cook the remaining 4 cutlets. Set the cutlets aside.

When buying veal, make sure it is either creamy white

In the same skillet, melt 1 more tablespoon of butter, then add the shallot and garlic, and sauté until fragrant, about 30 seconds. Add the mushrooms, ½ teaspoon of salt, and ¼ teaspoon of pepper, and sauté until the mushrooms are tender and the juices evaporate, about 3 minutes. Add the Marsala and rosemary sprig, and simmer until the Marsala reduces by half, about 2 minutes. Add the broth and simmer until reduced by half, about 4 minutes.

Working in batches, return the veal to the skillet and cook just until heated through, turning to coat, about 1 minute. Discard the rosemary sprig and stir the remaining 1 tablespoon of butter into the sauce. Season the sauce with more salt and pepper to taste.

Using tongs, transfer the veal to dinner plates. Spoon the sauce over the veal and serve.

or light pink, because it has the mildest flavor and is the freshest.

PORK MILANESE

These breaded cutlets are usually made with veal, but I've found that it's an excellent treatment for pork chops. As kids, my siblings and I loved this dish —what kids don't love fried meat? And it makes for a tasty sandwich the next day (see page 184).

4 MAIN-COURSE SERVINGS

⅓ cup all-purpose flour, for dredging

2 large eggs, beaten to blend

1¼ cups plain dried bread crumbs

⅔ cup grated Parmesan cheese

2 teaspoons dried basil

1 teaspoon dried thyme

4 8-ounce center-cut pork loin chops (each about 1 inch thick)

1 teaspoon salt, plus more to taste

1 teaspoon freshly ground black pepper

2 tablespoons butter

⅓ cup vegetable oil

1 lemon, cut into wedges

PLACE THE FLOUR in a wide, shallow bowl. Place the eggs in another wide, shallow bowl. Mix the bread crumbs, Parmesan cheese, basil, and thyme in a third wide, shallow bowl.

Using a meat mallet, pound the pork chops on the work surface until they are ¼ inch thick. Sprinkle the pork chops with 1 teaspoon each of salt and pepper. Working with one pork chop at a time, dredge the chops in the flour to coat lightly, then dip the chops into the beaten eggs, allowing the excess egg to drip off. Finally, coat the pork chops with the bread-crumb mixture, pressing gently to adhere. Set the pork chops in a single layer on a baking sheet. (The pork chops can be prepared up to this point 4 hours ahead. Cover and refrigerate.)

Preheat the oven to 150 degrees F. Line a baking sheet with a rack. In a large, heavy sauté pan with high sides, melt the butter in the oil over medium heat until hot. Carefully place 2 pork chops in the oil mixture and cook until light golden brown, about 3 minutes per side. Transfer the chops to the baking sheet and sprinkle with more salt to taste. Keep the cooked chops warm in the oven. Repeat with the remaining 2 chops.

Place 1 pork chop on each of 4 dinner plates, and serve immediately with the lemon wedges.

Don't be afraid of pounding pork, chicken, or veal. *It's easy, and pounding meat can be a great way to vent frustration. Place a boneless and, for chicken, skinless piece of meat between two pieces of plastic wrap and, using a mallet, lightly pound until approximately ½ inch thick. Your butcher can do this for you if you don't have the time. The advantage to pounding the meat thin is that the cooking process is quick and the meat doesn't have time to dry out.*

BRACIOLA

The word braciola *is used in different regions of Italy to describe different cuts of meat. But in southern Italy,* braciola *refers to a dish where a slice of meat is topped with different ingredients and rolled up and baked. It's moist, rich, and very flavorful, and it's actually easy to make, although not quick: In order to make this cut of meat moist and tasty, it needs a good amount of oven time. I like to serve it at holiday dinner parties or for Sunday supper.*

You will need kitchen twine to tie the rolled flank steak.

4 MAIN-COURSE SERVINGS

⅔ cup grated Pecorino Romano cheese

⅓ cup grated Provolone cheese

½ cup dried Italian-style bread crumbs

2 tablespoons chopped fresh flat-leaf parsley

1 garlic clove, minced

4 tablespoons olive oil

1 flank steak (1½ pounds)

1 teaspoon sea salt

1 teaspoon freshly ground black pepper

1 cup dry white wine

3¼ cups Marinara Sauce (page 59)

IN A MEDIUM BOWL, stir the cheeses, bread crumbs, parsley, and garlic to blend. Stir in 2 tablespoons of the oil, and set aside. Lay the flank steak flat on the work surface, and sprinkle with ½ teaspoon each of salt and pepper. Sprinkle the bread-crumb mixture evenly over the steak to cover the top evenly. Starting at one short end, roll up the steak as for a jelly roll and enclose the filling completely. Using kitchen twine, tie the steak roll to secure. Sprinkle the braciola with the remaining salt and pepper.

Preheat the oven to 350 degrees F. In a large, heavy, ovenproof frying pan, heat the remaining 2 tablespoons of oil over a medium flame. Add the braciola and cook until brown on all sides, about 8 minutes. Add the wine and bring to a boil. Stir in the marinara sauce. Cover partially with foil and bake, turning the braciola and basting with the sauce every

30 minutes, until the meat is almost tender, about 1½ hours. Uncover and continue baking until the meat is tender, about 30 minutes longer. (The braciola can be made up to this point 1 day ahead. Cool, then cover with foil and refrigerate. Rewarm in a 350 degree F oven until the braciola is heated through, about 30 minutes.)

Remove the braciola from the sauce. Using a large, sharp knife, remove the kitchen twine and cut the braciola crosswise and diagonally into ½-inch-thick slices. Transfer the slices to plates. Spoon the sauce over and serve.

You can be creative *with the flavorings. You can substitute mozzarella or even fontina or Gorgonzola; you can also use whatever herbs you like. Make this dish your own—that's what makes cooking so much fun.*

Everyday
ROASTS

Roasts are simple, satisfying, and great for guests; nearly all your work is done ahead of time. The key to roasting meats, whether chicken or fish or pork or beef, is to achieve the proper internal temperature for the type of meat. Cook it too long, and the meat's temperature gets too high, turning your roast dry and tough; not long enough, and it won't be safe to eat. But cook it just right, and you'll have a perfectly tender, flavorful, and downright easy entrée for a crowd. ▪ The secret to achieving the right internal temperature is simple: Use a meat thermometer. The basic models cost just a couple of bucks, but I'm in love with my electronic one: The sensor stays in the oven, inserted into the meat, while a wire extends to the readout on my stovetop, and it has an alarm that lets me know when the meat has reached the desired temperature.

Here are the proper internal temperatures of meats:

Fresh beef, veal, and lamb	145 degrees F	medium-rare
Fresh pork	170 degrees F	well done
Fresh chicken and turkey	180 degrees F or until juices run clear	well done

ROASTED RED SNAPPER
with Rosemary

Roasting fish is easy and helps keep it moist, tender, and flaky. On Italy's many coasts, it's popular to cook fish whole—including tail and head, which is considered a delicacy for many types of fish. I can live without the heads, but I do like to stuff the fish for an added burst of flavor and aroma.

4 MAIN-COURSE SERVINGS

2 tablespoons olive oil

1 whole red snapper (about 3 pounds), cleaned and scaled

1 teaspoon salt, plus more to taste

1 teaspoon freshly ground black pepper, plus more to taste

1 lemon, cut into 8 wedges

½ small onion, coarsely chopped

½ fennel bulb, coarsely chopped

6 sprigs of fresh rosemary

2 garlic cloves, thinly sliced

PREHEAT THE OVEN to 400 degrees F. Line a large, heavy baking sheet with foil. Coat the foil with 1 tablespoon of the oil. Place the fish atop the foil, and sprinkle the fish cavity with ½ teaspoon each of salt and pepper. Squeeze the juice from 4 lemon wedges inside the fish cavity and then place those wedges in the cavity. Fill the cavity with the onion, fennel, rosemary, and garlic. Rub the remaining 1 tablespoon of oil over the fish and sprinkle with ½ teaspoon each of salt and pepper. (The fish can be prepared up to this point 6 hours ahead. Cover and refrigerate. Uncover before baking.)

Roast in the oven until the fish is just cooked through at the bone, about 40 minutes. Pull back the skin from atop the fish. Using a sharp knife, separate the two fillets from the backbone. Using a metal spatula, transfer the fillets to plates. Lift the fish backbone from the bottom fillets (the backbone and head should come off together easily), and discard. Using the spatula, transfer the remaining two fillets to plates. Sprinkle the fish with more salt and pepper to taste, and serve with the remaining lemon wedges.

SALMON BAKED IN FOIL

Cooking fish al cartoccio—literally, "in a bag"—is a technique that's been used by Italians (and other cultures) for a long time. It's actually a method of steaming rather than baking; the tight wrapping seals in all the juices and aromas so you end up with a mouthwatering combination of flavors. Traditionally, the fish is wrapped in parchment paper, but I like to use aluminum foil because it's easier to close tightly. (It's not as pretty or traditional as parchment paper, but aluminum foil is one modern convenience that I'm just not willing to forgo for the sake of prettiness or tradition.) You can cook almost any fish you want in foil or parchment, and indeed in Italy it's usually used for swordfish and sea bass, not salmon, which doesn't swim in the Mediterranean; but I love salmon's creaminess and year-round availability, so I've taken my liberties with the al cartoccio tradition. This method also produces superb vegetables and chicken. And a bonus: It's mess-free.

4 MAIN-COURSE SERVINGS

 3 tomatoes, chopped, or 1 (14-ounce) can diced tomatoes in juice, drained

 2 shallots, chopped

 2 tablespoons plus 2 teaspoons olive oil

 2 tablespoons fresh lemon juice (from about ½ lemon)

1½ teaspoons chopped fresh oregano or ¾ teaspoon dried

1½ teaspoons chopped fresh thyme or ¾ teaspoon dried

 1 teaspoon salt

¾ teaspoon freshly ground black pepper

 4 salmon fillets (about 5 ounces each)

PREHEAT THE OVEN to 400 degrees F. In a medium bowl, stir the tomatoes, shallots, 2 tablespoons of oil, lemon juice, oregano, thyme, ½ teaspoon of salt, and ¼ teaspoon of pepper. In the center of each of four large sheets of aluminum foil, spoon ½ teaspoon of oil. Place 1 salmon fillet atop each sheet of foil and turn to coat with the oil. Sprinkle the salmon fillets with the remaining ½ teaspoon each of salt and pepper. Spoon the tomato mixture over the salmon. Fold the sides of the foil over the fish and tomato mixture, covering completely, and seal the packets closed. Place the foil packets on a large, heavy baking sheet. (The salmon packets can be prepared up to this point 6 hours ahead. Refrigerate until ready to bake.)

Bake until the salmon is just cooked through, about 25 minutes. Using a large metal spatula, transfer the foil packets to plates and serve. (You may want to unwrap and plate the fish in the kitchen before serving.)

ROASTED PORK LOIN
with Fig Sauce

This dish is perfect for entertaining a large group because it serves a crowd and looks spectacular, and the rich, velvety fig sauce will knock your guests' socks off; it's so sweet you could even serve it over ice cream. Many European cultures have traditional recipes that pair pork with sweet fruit, usually apples. But apples aren't so prevalent in Italy, and figs are. Lucky for Italians.

4 TO 6 MAIN-COURSE SERVINGS

Fig Sauce

2½ cups port

1¼ cups reduced-sodium chicken broth

8 dried black Mission figs, coarsely chopped

2 sprigs of fresh rosemary

2 cinnamon sticks

1 tablespoon honey

2 tablespoons unsalted butter, cut into pieces

¼ teaspoon salt

¼ teaspoon freshly ground black pepper

Pork

2 tablespoons olive oil

2 tablespoons chopped fresh rosemary

1 tablespoon salt, plus more to taste

1½ teaspoons freshly ground black pepper, plus more to taste

1 4- to 4½-pound boneless pork loin

1 cup low-sodium chicken broth

FOR THE FIG SAUCE

In a medium-size, heavy saucepan, combine the port, chicken broth, figs, rosemary, cinnamon, and honey. Boil over medium-high heat until reduced by half, about 30 minutes. Discard the rosemary sprigs and cinnamon sticks (some of the rosemary leaves will remain in the port mixture). Transfer the port mixture to a blender and purée until smooth. Blend in the butter, salt, and pepper. (The sauce can be made 1 day ahead. Cover and refrigerate. Rewarm over medium heat before using.)

FOR THE PORK

Preheat the oven to 425 degrees F. Stir the oil, rosemary, 1 tablespoon of salt, and 1½ teaspoons of pepper in a small bowl to blend. Place the pork

(recipe continues)

loin in a heavy, flame-proof roasting pan. Spread the oil mixture over the pork to coat completely. Roast, turning the pork every 15 minutes to ensure even browning, until an instant-read meat thermometer inserted into the center of the pork registers 145 degrees F, about 45 minutes total.

Transfer the pork to a cutting board and tent with foil to keep warm. Let the pork rest for 15 minutes. Meanwhile, place the roasting pan over medium heat and stir in the chicken broth, scraping the bottom of the pan to remove any browned bits. Bring the pan juices to a simmer. Season with more salt and pepper to taste.

Using a large, sharp knife, cut the pork crosswise into ¼-inch-thick slices. Arrange the pork slices on plates. Spoon the jus over. Drizzle the warm fig sauce around and serve immediately.

ROASTED CHICKEN
with Balsamic Vinaigrette

If you're bored with the same old roast chicken, try this one. The bird absorbs all the sweet and savory flavors of the marinade, and that's what keeps the meat incredibly moist. And it's still moist the next day—perfect for sandwiches and salads. This is a really easy recipe to double (as long as you have a big enough roasting pan). So I usually do, and enjoy my leftovers all week.

4 MAIN-COURSE SERVINGS

½ cup balsamic vinegar

¼ cup fresh lemon juice (from about 1 lemon)

¼ cup Dijon mustard

3 garlic cloves, minced

1 teaspoon salt

1 teaspoon freshly ground black pepper

½ cup olive oil

Chicken, cut into 6 pieces (about 4 pounds; reserve giblets, neck, and backbone for another use)

1 tablespoon chopped fresh flat-leaf parsley

1 teaspoon grated lemon zest (from about 1 lemon)

IN A 13 × 9 × 2-INCH BAKING DISH, whisk the vinegar, lemon juice, mustard, garlic, salt, and pepper to blend. Whisk in the oil. Add the chicken pieces and turn to coat. Cover and refrigerate, turning the chicken pieces occasionally, for at least 2 hours and up to 1 day.

Preheat the oven to 400 degrees F. Roast the chicken uncovered until just cooked through, about 45 minutes. Using tongs, transfer the chicken to a serving platter. Carefully pour the cooking liquid into a small, heavy saucepan and spoon off the excess oil from atop the cooking liquid. Boil until the liquid reduces by about half and thickens slightly, about 8 minutes.

Pour the sauce over the chicken. Sprinkle the parsley and lemon zest over the chicken, and serve.

If the chicken gets too dark too quickly, cover it with aluminum foil, taking the foil off for the last 10 minutes of roasting.

TURKEY TONNATO

I freely admit that the tonnato preparation is an idea that takes some getting used to: It means that a meat, usually veal, is topped with tuna sauce—and it's usually served cold. But before you say "Ugh" and turn the page, please give it a try. It's really a wonderful combination of flavors. Instead of veal, I prefer the lighter taste of turkey paired with the relatively strong sauce, and I like this dish warm, not cold.

2 MAIN-COURSE SERVINGS

1 skinless boneless turkey breast (about ½ pound)

2 tablespoons extra-virgin olive oil

1 tablespoon dried oregano

1 tablespoon dried thyme

1 tablespoon dried basil

1 teaspoon salt, plus more to taste

1 teaspoon freshly ground black pepper, plus more to taste

2 cups plus 1 tablespoon reduced-sodium chicken broth

4 ounces canned tuna, packed in olive oil (do not drain)

1 tablespoon fresh lemon juice (from about ½ lemon)

1 tablespoon drained capers

1 teaspoon anchovy paste or 1 anchovy fillet, drained

⅓ cup mayonnaise

1 tablespoon chopped fresh flat-leaf parsley

PREHEAT THE OVEN to 375 degrees F. Place the turkey in a baking pan and rub the oil over the turkey. Sprinkle with the dried herbs and 1 teaspoon each of salt and pepper. Pour 2 cups of the broth around the turkey and bake until it is just cooked through, about 30 minutes. Let the turkey cool in the pan for 10 minutes, then transfer the turkey to a cutting board. Using a large, sharp knife, cut the turkey diagonally into ½-inch-thick slices. Return the turkey slices to the baking pan and coat with the pan juices.

In the bowl of a food processor, blend the tuna, lemon juice, capers, anchovy paste, and the remaining 1 tablespoon of broth until creamy, about 1 minute. Transfer the tuna mixture to a medium bowl, and stir in the mayonnaise. Season the tuna sauce with salt and pepper to taste.

Arrange the turkey slices on a platter and pour the tuna sauce over. Garnish with the parsley and serve.

AUNT RAFFY'S TURKEY STUFFING

I'm not going to tell you that this is a traditional dish from Umbria; it's not. But it is a traditional dish in my family. And family is what tradition is all about, isn't it?

1 medium Granny Smith apple, cored and cut into 1-inch cubes

1 medium Red Delicious apple, cored and cut into 1-inch cubes

1 medium onion, chopped

1 tablespoon vegetable oil

1½ tablespoons unsalted butter

1 (6-ounce) bag dried cranberries

¼ cup dry white wine

1½ teaspoons salt, plus more to taste

1 teaspoon freshly ground black pepper, plus more to taste

1 pound sweet Italian turkey sausages, casings removed

1 (7.25-ounce) jar steamed whole chestnuts, coarsely chopped

8 ounces day-old cornbread or bread, cut into 1-inch cubes

1 cup canned chicken broth

1 cup freshly grated Parmesan cheese

PREHEAT THE OVEN to 400 degrees F. In a medium pot, cook the apples, onion, oil, and 1 tablespoon of the butter over medium-low heat until the apples soften, about 10 minutes. Add the cranberries and wine and simmer until the wine evaporates and the cranberries are tender, about 5 minutes. Stir in the salt and pepper. Let cool.

In a large, heavy sauté pan, cook the sausages over medium-high heat until browned and cooked through, breaking them up with a wooden spoon, about 8 minutes. Lightly coat an 8½-inch square baking dish with ½ tablespoon of butter. In a medium bowl, combine the apple mixture, sausage, chestnuts, and cornbread. Gently stir in the broth and ¾ cup of the Parmesan. Season with salt and pepper. Transfer to the baking dish and sprinkle with ¼ cup of Parmesan. Bake until the top is golden brown and the stuffing is heated through, about 45 minutes.

Everyday
STEWS AND SAUCES

Something wonderfully fragrant is bubbling away in the oven, infus-

ing your home with the inviting aromas of tomato, garlic, and onion;

these are the dishes that take you back to Grandma's Sunday sup-

pers. But while Grandma may have slaved all day, you don't have to.

In the following recipes, I've streamlined the traditional long-

simmered stews and sauced entrées to help get you out of the

kitchen, and dinner onto the table, on an *Everyday Italian* timetable.

So invite Grandma over and return the favor after all these years.

CHICKEN SPEZZATINO

Italian stews are called spezzatini *because the meat is cut into pieces;* spezzare *means "to cut up" or "break up." This is the prototypical one-pot meal: Throw all the ingredients into a pot, and you have a great dinner.*

4 TO 6 MAIN-COURSE SERVINGS

2 tablespoons olive oil

2 celery stalks, cut into bite-size pieces

1 carrot, peeled and cut into bite-size pieces

1 small onion, chopped

1 teaspoon salt, plus more to taste

1 teaspoon freshly ground black pepper, plus more to taste

1 (14½-ounce) can chopped tomatoes with their juices

1 (14-ounce) can reduced-sodium chicken broth

½ cup fresh basil leaves, torn into pieces

1 tablespoon tomato paste

1 bay leaf

½ teaspoon dried thyme

2 chicken breasts with ribs (about 1½ pounds total)

1 (15-ounce) can organic kidney beans, drained (rinsed if not organic)

IN A HEAVY 5½-quart saucepan, heat the oil over a medium flame. Add the celery, carrot, and onion, and sauté until the onion is translucent, about 5 minutes. Add the salt and pepper. Stir in the tomatoes, broth, basil, tomato paste, bay leaf, and thyme. Add the chicken and press to submerge. Bring the liquid to a simmer. Reduce the heat to medium-low and simmer gently, uncovered, turning the breasts over and stirring occasionally, until the chicken is almost cooked through, about 20 minutes. Add the kidney beans and simmer until the chicken is cooked through and the liquid has reduced to a stew consistency, about 10 minutes.

Discard the bay leaf. Let the chicken cool for 5 minutes. Discard the skin and bones and cut the meat into bite-size pieces. Return it to the stew and bring to a simmer. Add salt and pepper to taste.

CHICKEN CACCIATORE

Cacciatore *means cooked in the "hunter's style" (which, translated into French, is* chasseur *and in fact refers to a very similar dish). In many Italian-American restaurants this can be a greasy, overly sweet sauce with dry, overcooked chicken. But this recipe will make you fall in love with Chicken Cacciatore again; it's really the ultimate in hearty, rustic Italian home cooking.*

4 MAIN-COURSE SERVINGS

- 4 chicken thighs
- 2 chicken breasts with skin and backbone, halved crosswise
- 2 teaspoons salt, plus more to taste
- 1 teaspoon freshly ground black pepper, plus more to taste
- ½ cup all-purpose flour, for dredging
- 3 tablespoons olive oil
- 1 large red bell pepper, chopped
- 1 onion, chopped
- 6 garlic cloves, finely chopped
- 1½ teaspoons dried oregano leaves
- ¾ cup dry white wine
- 1 (28-ounce) can diced tomatoes with juice
- ¾ cup reduced-sodium chicken broth
- 3 tablespoons drained capers
- ¼ cup coarsely chopped fresh basil

SPRINKLE THE CHICKEN PIECES with 1 teaspoon each of salt and pepper. Dredge the chicken pieces in the flour to coat lightly.

In a large, heavy sauté pan, heat the oil over a medium-high flame. Working in 2 batches, add the chicken pieces to the pan and sauté just until brown, about 5 minutes per side. Transfer the chicken to a plate and set aside. Add the bell pepper, onion, garlic, and oregano to the same pan and sauté over medium heat until the onion is tender, about 5 minutes.

(recipe continues)

Add the wine and simmer until reduced by half, about 3 minutes. Add the tomatoes with their juice, broth, and capers. Return the chicken pieces to the pan and turn them to coat in the sauce. Bring the sauce to a simmer. Continue simmering over medium-low heat until the chicken is just cooked through, about 20 minutes for the breast pieces, and 30 minutes for the thighs.

Using tongs, transfer the chicken to a platter. If necessary, boil the sauce until it thickens slightly, about 3 minutes. Spoon off any excess fat from atop the sauce. Spoon the sauce over the chicken, then sprinkle with the basil and serve.

Stewing and braising *are cooking techniques that deliver moist, tender meat. The slow cooking process allows all the flavors to intermingle and create a rich sauce.*

SHRIMP FRA DIAVOLO

Fra Diavolo means "Brother Devil." In Italy, this refers to a dish that's sprinkled heavily with black pepper and grilled. But in America the term is associated with spicy hot-pepper sauces, like the lobster Fra Diavolo that became popular in the 1930s and has been a fixture on Italian-American menus ever since. (It is actually unknown in Italy, where they don't have the same type of lobsters we do.) I make my version of Fra Diavolo with shrimp because it's lighter and easier for everyday cooking.

4 MAIN-COURSE SERVINGS

1 pound large shrimp, peeled and deveined

1 teaspoon salt, plus more to taste

1 teaspoon dried crushed red pepper flakes

3 tablespoons olive oil

1 medium onion, finely chopped

1 (14½-ounce) can diced tomatoes with juices

1 cup dry white wine

3 garlic cloves, chopped

¼ teaspoon dried oregano leaves

3 tablespoons chopped fresh flat-leaf parsley

3 tablespoons chopped fresh basil

IN A MEDIUM BOWL, toss the shrimp with 1 teaspoon of the salt and the red pepper flakes. In a large, heavy skillet, heat the oil over a medium-high flame. Add the shrimp and sauté until just cooked through, about 2 minutes. Using a slotted spoon, transfer the shrimp to a large plate and set aside. Add the onion to the same skillet and sauté until translucent, about 5 minutes. Add the tomatoes with their juices, wine, garlic, and oregano, and simmer until the sauce thickens slightly, about 10 minutes. Return the shrimp and any accumulated juices to the tomato mixture and toss to coat. Remove from the heat and stir in the parsley and basil. Season with more salt to taste. Spoon the shrimp mixture into shallow bowls and serve.

MUSSELS, CLAMS, AND SHRIMP
in Spicy Tomato Broth

The clam and mussel soups that are specialties of Naples and the nearby coastlines inspired this recipe. I've added shrimp for more meatiness and dried crushed red pepper flakes simply because I like it spicy, but they're optional. Whatever you do, be sure to serve this with plenty of crusty bread; the broth is phenomenal to sop up.

6 MAIN-COURSE SERVINGS

¼ cup olive oil

5 garlic cloves, minced

1 bay leaf

1 teaspoon dried crushed red pepper flakes

1 cup dry white wine

1 (28-ounce) can diced tomatoes with juices

24 small littleneck clams (about 2½ pounds total), scrubbed

24 mussels (about 1½ pounds total), debearded

20 large shrimp (about 1 pound), peeled, deveined, and butterflied

½ cup torn fresh basil leaves

  Warm crusty bread, to serve

IN A LARGE, wide pot, heat the oil over a medium flame. Add the garlic, bay leaf, and red pepper flakes, and sauté until the garlic is tender, about 1 minute. Add the wine and bring to a boil. Add the tomatoes with their juices and simmer, stirring often, until the tomatoes begin to break down and the flavors blend, about 8 minutes. Stir in the clams, then cover and cook for 5 minutes. Stir in the mussels, then cover and continue cooking until the clams and mussels open, about 5 minutes longer.

Using tongs, transfer the opened shellfish to serving bowls (discard any shellfish that do not open). Add the shrimp to the simmering tomato broth, and simmer until the shrimp are just cooked through, about 1½ minutes. Stir in the basil. Remove the bay leaf. Divide the shrimp and tomato broth among the bowls, and serve with the warm bread.

The **trick** to this dish is to be careful not to overcook the shellfish—otherwise, it will become rubbery.

EASY OSSO BUCO

Osso buco is braised veal shanks. The fabulously flavorful veal shanks are cooked for a long time, making the meat so tender that it literally falls off the bones. I'm not sure why, but I think people are afraid of this dish; maybe they're intimidated by the unfamiliarity of veal shanks. But it's really easy to prepare and just needs a couple of hours to cook, while the fragrant aromas fill your house and maybe even tempt the neighbors to ring the doorbell to find out what's cooking. The perfect dish for a rainy Sunday.

Be sure to have kitchen twine available for tying the shanks.

6 MAIN-COURSE SERVINGS

6 1- to 1½-inch-thick slices veal shank (about 14 ounces each)

2½ teaspoons salt, plus more to taste

1½ teaspoons freshly ground black pepper, plus more to taste

⅓ cup all-purpose flour, for dredging

¼ cup vegetable oil

1 small onion, finely chopped

1 small carrot, finely chopped

1 celery stalk, finely chopped

1 tablespoon tomato paste

1 cup dry white wine

   About 4 cups reduced-sodium chicken broth

1 large sprig of fresh rosemary

1 large sprig of fresh thyme

1 bay leaf

2 whole cloves

1 tablespoon chopped fresh flat-leaf parsley

PREHEAT THE OVEN to 375 degrees F. Pat the veal dry with paper towels to ensure even browning. Secure the meat to the bone with kitchen twine. Season the veal with 1½ teaspoons each of salt and pepper. Dredge the veal in the flour to coat the cut sides lightly.

In a heavy roasting pan large enough to fit the veal in a single layer, heat the oil over a medium flame until hot. Add the veal and cook until brown on both sides, about 8 minutes per side. Transfer the veal to a plate and reserve.

In the same pan, add the onion, carrot, and celery. Season with 1 teaspoon of salt to help draw out the moisture from the vegetables. Sauté until the onion is tender, about 6 minutes. Stir in the tomato paste and sauté for 1 minute. Stir in the wine and simmer until the liquid is reduced by half, about 2 minutes. Return the veal to the pan. Add enough chicken broth to come two thirds of the way up the sides of the veal. Add the herb sprigs, bay leaf, and cloves to the broth mixture. Bring the liquid to a boil over medium-high heat. Remove the pan from the heat. Cover the pan with foil and transfer to the oven. Braise until the veal is fork-tender, turning the veal every 30 minutes, about 1½ hours total.

Carefully remove the cooked veal from the pan and transfer to a cutting board. Cut off the twine and discard. Tent the veal with foil to keep warm.

Place a large sieve over a large bowl. Carefully pour the cooking liquid and vegetables into the sieve, pressing on the solids to release as much liquid as possible. Discard the solids and return the sauce to the pan. Gently place the veal back into the strained sauce. Bring just to a simmer. Season the sauce with more salt and pepper to taste. (The osso buco can be prepared to this point up to 1 day ahead. Cool, then cover and refrigerate. Keep covered and rewarm in a 350 degree F oven until the veal is heated through, about 25 minutes.) Place one veal shank on each plate and spoon the sauce over. Garnish with the parsley and serve.

Everyday
LEFTOVERS

When I'm having people over for dinner, I almost always make too much—better too much than too little, right? So the next night, I look in my fridge and see the leftovers: that leftover half-steak, or breaded veal cutlet, or small bowl of grilled seafood from my seafood salad. But do I really want to have the same meal tonight that I had last night? No. So instead of just reheating my leftovers and having dinner déjà vu, I figure out a way to use those leftovers as an ingredient in something new. The half-steak becomes a delicious steak salad, the cutlet becomes one of the best sandwiches you can imagine, and the seafood turns an ordinary side-dish risotto into a main-dish centerpiece.

STEAK SALAD

The beauty of a dish like this is that you get just enough meat to feel satisfied that you've had a substantial meal, but you've actually consumed a much greater proportion of healthy greens than of red meat. Plus, it can serve four people on the budget of one steak.

4 MAIN-COURSE SERVINGS

½   head of romaine lettuce, cut into bite-size pieces

2   large heads of Belgian endive, thinly sliced crosswise (about 3 cups)

3   cups fresh baby arugula

12   cherry tomatoes, halved

½   red onion, thinly sliced into rings

4   ounces Gorgonzola cheese, coarsely crumbled

Red Wine Vinaigrette (page 184)

About ¼ teaspoon salt

About ¼ teaspoon freshly ground black pepper

1   pound leftover steak (such as New York, rib eye, or filet mignon), cut crosswise into thin slices

IN A LARGE BOWL, toss the lettuce, endive, arugula, tomatoes, and onion to combine. Add half of the cheese and toss the salad with enough vinaigrette to coat. Season the salad with salt and pepper to taste. Divide the salad equally among 4 plates and top with the steak slices. Drizzle more vinaigrette over the steak slices and sprinkle with the remaining cheese. Serve immediately.

RED WINE VINAIGRETTE

A simple, light, and versatile dressing that can be used to top any salad. The honey adds a little sweetness and rounds out the flavors.

MAKES 1²/₃ CUPS

½ cup red wine vinegar

3 tablespoons lemon juice

2 teaspoons honey

2 teaspoons salt, plus more to taste

1 cup olive oil

Freshly ground black pepper

Mix the vinegar, lemon juice, honey, and 2 teaspoons salt in a blender. With the machine running, gradually blend in the oil. Season the vinaigrette with salt and pepper to taste.

MILANESE SANDWICH

This sandwich can be made with any meat prepared in the Milanese style (see recipe on page 158)—veal, chicken, or pork. You can use whatever ingredients you want, but the combination below tastes great.

SERVES 2

2 Italian or French rolls (each about 6 inches long), halved horizontally

½ ripe avocado, peeled, pitted, and sliced

2 teaspoons extra-virgin olive oil

1 teaspoon balsamic vinegar

1 generous pinch of salt

1 generous pinch of freshly ground black pepper

1 medium tomato, sliced

²/₃ cup arugula leaves

1 cooked Pork Milanese cutlet (page 158), warm or cold, cut into thin slices

WITH YOUR FINGERS, remove and discard some of the soft inner bread from the rolls, creating a shallow well in each. Divide the avocado among all 4 pieces of bread. Using a fork, mash the avocado over the bread.

In a medium bowl, whisk the oil, vinegar, salt, and pepper to blend. Add the tomato and arugula and toss to coat. Divide the arugula mixture between the 2 bottom pieces of bread, add the sliced Pork Milanese, and cover with the top pieces of bread. Cut the sandwiches in half and serve.

GRILLED-SEAFOOD RISOTTO

I serve most risottos as a side dish, but this is an entrée-style risotto. With a fresh green salad and a glass of crisp Pinot Grigio, this is one of my favorite light suppers—and it's based on leftovers!

2 MAIN-COURSE SERVINGS

½ recipe Basic Risotto (page 128)

½ cup (or more) chicken broth

1 to 2 cups grilled scallops and squid, from Grilled Seafood Salad (page 143)

2 tablespoons chopped fresh flat-leaf parsley

IN A HEAVY, medium-size saucepan, stir the risotto and ½ cup of broth over a medium flame until the mixture is heated through. Add the grilled scallops and squid and any additional broth to loosen slightly. Continue cooking the risotto, stirring gently to avoid breaking up the scallops, until the seafood is just heated through. Stir in the parsley. Transfer the risotto to serving bowls and serve immediately.

everyday

contorni

EVERYDAY STUFFED VEGETABLES

Stuffed Mushrooms ▪ Eggplant Rollatini ▪
Stuffed Tomatoes

ROASTED AND BAKED

Tomato Vegetable Casserole ▪ Verdure al Forno ▪
Roasted Baby Potatoes with Herbs and Garlic ▪
Herb-Roasted Root Vegetables

QUICK AND SIMPLE

Peas and Prosciutto ▪ Sautéed Broccoli Rabe with
Raisins and Pine Nuts ▪ Brussels Sprouts with
Pancetta ▪ Everyday Caponata ▪ Broccoli and Green
Beans ▪ Smashed Parmesan Potatoes ▪ Grilled
Vegetables

EVERYDAY SALADS

Endive and Frisée Salad with Blood Oranges and
Hazelnuts ▪ Farro Salad with Tomatoes and Herbs ▪
Panzanella

EVERYDAY
STUFFED VEGETABLES

An Italian dinner isn't complete without a side vegetable dish—the contorno. Some of my favorite vegetable dishes are stuffed, which traditionally was a way for home cooks to use up their leftovers. Italians eat a lot of bread and cook a lot of grains, especially rice and, of course, pasta. But what do you do with a few pieces of stale bread? Or a cup of leftover rice? Ever-resourceful Italian house-wives used these small portions to round out the next night's dinner by making stuffings—sometimes for meats, sometimes for vegetables. But whether the stuffing is made from leftovers or from scratch, these not only make great *contorni* but also perfect main courses for vegetarian meals. And they look great, too. ▪ Another benefit of stuffed vegetables is that baked ones can be assembled ahead of time. When your guests arrive, just pop the casserole in the oven, and it'll be ready by the time you've gobbled down your antipasti. And some stuffed-vegetable recipes can—and maybe even should—be eaten at room temperature, which is perhaps the all-time greatest benefit you can ask of a recipe when you're feeding a crowd.

STUFFED MUSHROOMS

In Italy, one of the most popular recipes for stuffed mushrooms hails from Liguria, the northern region that stretches along the Mediterranean coast (actually, the body of water here is called the Ligurian Sea) from the border of France all the way down to Tuscany. The capital of the region is Genoa, which on the one hand is the birthplace of pesto, and on the other is a port city where seafood is worked into recipes where you wouldn't necessarily expect it. Like mushrooms, for example, which they stuff with salted anchovies, marjoram, and bread crumbs. That recipe is a little complex, so I've omitted the little fishes and simplified. This is not only a great side dish, but also the perfect antipasto for a casual get-together.

MAKES 28 MUSHROOMS

½   cup Italian-style dried bread crumbs

½   cup freshly grated Pecorino Romano cheese

2   tablespoon chopped fresh flat-leaf parsley

1   tablespoon chopped fresh mint

2   garlic cloves, minced

     About 3 tablespoons olive oil

28   large (2½-inch-diameter) white mushrooms, stemmed

PREHEAT THE OVEN to 400 degrees F. In a medium bowl, stir the bread crumbs, Romano cheese, parsley, mint, and garlic to blend.

Lightly coat a large, heavy baking sheet with 2 teaspoons of the oil. Arrange the mushroom caps on the baking sheet, cavity side up, and spoon the filling into the mushroom cavities. Drizzle ¼ teaspoon of oil over the filling in each mushroom. Bake until the mushrooms are tender and the filling is heated through and golden on top, about 25 minutes. Arrange the stuffed mushrooms on a platter and serve.

EGGPLANT ROLLATINI

Eggplant Parmesan is one of the classic red-checkered-tablecloth Italian-American recipes, but I prefer this slightly easier and lighter recipe, with a very similar concept—combining eggplant with cheese and marinara sauce. This makes an elegant, satisfying side dish as well as a great entrée for a vegetarian meal (make sure your vegetarians eat dairy, though—there's lots of it here). You could also make this dish with zucchini.

6 SIDE-DISH SERVINGS

4 medium eggplants (about 4 pounds), cut lengthwise into ½-inch-thick slices

1 tablespoon plus 1 teaspoon sea salt

½ cup extra-virgin olive oil, plus more for drizzling

3 tablespoons pine nuts

32 ounces whole-milk ricotta cheese

2 large eggs, beaten to blend

½ cup shredded mozzarella cheese

3 tablespoons freshly grated Parmesan cheese

20 basil leaves, very thinly sliced

2 cups Marinara Sauce (page 59)

1 teaspoon freshly ground black pepper

ARRANGE THE EGGPLANT SLICES over a large baking sheet and sprinkle with 1 tablespoon of salt (this will help extract the moisture from the eggplant). Set the eggplant aside for 15 minutes. Rinse the eggplant to remove the salt, and pat dry.

Prepare a charcoal or gas grill for medium heat, or preheat a ridged grill pan over a medium flame. Brush the eggplant slices with ½ cup of oil and grill until lightly browned and tender, about 4 minutes per side.

Preheat the oven to 375 degrees F. Place the pine nuts on a heavy baking sheet, and toast in the oven, stirring once, until the nuts are fragrant and light golden brown, about 5 minutes. Let cool. Maintain the oven temperature.

Lightly oil a $13 \times 9 \times 2$-inch baking dish. In a large bowl, mix the ricotta cheese and eggs to blend. Gently stir in the mozzarella cheese, Parmesan cheese, and toasted pine nuts. Fold in the basil just to combine (do not overmix). Place 1 tablespoon of the cheese mixture at one short end of each eggplant slice and roll up tightly. Place the eggplant rollatini seam side down in the prepared baking dish. (The eggplant rollatini can be prepared up to this point 8 hours ahead. Cover and refrigerate.) Spoon the marinara sauce evenly over the eggplant rollatini and sprinkle with 1 teaspoon each of salt and pepper. Bake uncovered until the eggplant rollatini are heated through, about 15 minutes. Drizzle more oil over the eggplant rollatini and serve.

Cooking the rice ahead of time helps the tomato keep its shape when it's baked. And so the presentation is better.

STUFFED TOMATOES

I often serve these tomatoes at room temperature, and believe me, it's a real relief to be able to serve a dish to which you have to do absolutely nothing while your guests are in your home, other than put it on a plate. That's truly Everyday Italian cooking.

4 SIDE-DISH SERVINGS

Salt

⅔ cup Arborio rice or medium-grain white rice

1 teaspoon plus 2 tablespoons olive oil

4 ripe but firm large tomatoes

3 tablespoons chopped fresh basil

2 tablespoons chopped fresh flat-leaf parsley

1 garlic clove, minced

½ teaspoon freshly ground black pepper, plus more to taste

¼ cup freshly grated Parmesan cheese

BRING A MEDIUM SAUCEPAN of salted water to a boil. Add the rice and simmer over medium heat until just cooked through, stirring occasionally, about 10 minutes. Drain and rinse the rice under cold running water. Drain well. Transfer the rice to a medium bowl and set aside.

Preheat the oven to 350 degrees F. Lightly coat an 8-inch square baking dish with 1 teaspoon of oil. Cut a ½-inch-thick slice off the top of each tomato; reserve the tops. Scoop the seeds, pulp, and juice from each into a small bowl. Place the hollowed tomatoes in the prepared dish.

Add ¼ cup of the tomato pulp to the rice and toss to coat. Stir in the basil, parsley, garlic, remaining 2 tablespoons of oil, and ½ teaspoon each of salt and pepper. Stir in the Parmesan and season with more salt and pepper to taste. Spoon the rice mixture into the hollowed tomatoes, mounding slightly. Replace the reserved tops and bake until the rice is heated through, about 20 minutes. Serve hot or at room temperature. (The stuffed tomatoes can be made up to 4 hours ahead.)

ROASTED AND BAKED

I love roasting vegetables for two reasons: First, the flavor can't be beat—the natural sugars of the veggies intensify in the oven, and this sweetness transforms everyday produce into nearly dessert-like treats. Second, roasting vegetables is a very do-ahead preparation; I can do nearly all my kitchen labor ahead of time, letting the oven work while I relax and sip a glass of wine.

TOMATO VEGETABLE CASSEROLE

Note that the ingredients here are something of a hodgepodge: potato and sweet potato, zucchini and carrot, onion and bell pepper. That's because this is a pretty loose recipe, and you should feel free to substitute whatever you prefer. Just be sure to cut any vegetables to roughly the same size, to ensure that they're all fully cooked—but not overcooked—at the same time.

6 SIDE-DISH SERVINGS

1 medium potato, peeled and cut into ½-inch pieces

1 medium sweet potato, peeled and cut into ½-inch pieces

2 carrots, peeled and cut into ½-inch pieces

1 red bell pepper, cored, seeded, and cut into ½-inch pieces

4 tablespoons olive oil

1¾ teaspoons freshly ground black pepper

1½ teaspoons salt

½ red onion, thinly sliced into rings

1 large zucchini, cut crosswise into ¼-inch-thick slices

2 large ripe tomatoes, cut crosswise into ¼-inch-thick slices

½ cup freshly grated Parmesan cheese

2 tablespoons Italian-style dried bread crumbs

Sprigs of fresh basil, for garnish

PREHEAT THE OVEN to 450 degrees F. In a 13×9×2-inch glass baking dish, toss the potato, sweet potato, carrots, bell pepper, 2 tablespoons of the oil, ¾ teaspoon of pepper, and ½ teaspoon of salt. Arrange the onion evenly on top, then top with the zucchini. Drizzle with 1 tablespoon of the oil and sprinkle with ½ teaspoon each of salt and pepper. Arrange the tomato slices over the zucchini. Drizzle with the remaining 1 tablespoon of oil and sprinkle with the remaining ½ teaspoon each of salt and pepper.

In a small bowl, stir the Parmesan and bread crumbs to blend and sprinkle over the vegetables. Bake uncovered until the vegetables are tender and the topping is golden brown, about 40 minutes. Let cool for 10 minutes. Garnish with fresh basil sprigs and serve.

VERDURE AL FORNO

Even though this dish uses only zucchini, my grandmother called it Verdure al Forno, *which means "vegetables in the oven." (So it should really be called* Zucchine al Forno, *but there was absolutely no way anybody would tell that to my grandmother.) You could substitute eggplant, summer squash, potatoes, or even cauliflower for the zucchini, and make this your very own Verdure al Forno.*

4 SIDE-DISH SERVINGS

2 teaspoons extra-virgin olive oil

5 medium zucchini (about 1½ pounds total), cut crosswise into 1-inch-thick slices

½ teaspoon salt, plus more to taste

½ teaspoon freshly ground black pepper, plus more to taste

1 cup heavy cream

1 cup grated mozzarella cheese

1 cup grated fontina cheese

6 tablespoons grated Pecorino Romano cheese

1 cup plain dried bread crumbs

PREHEAT THE OVEN to 350 degrees F. Line a baking sheet with foil. Coat the bottom of an 8-inch square baking dish with the oil. Arrange enough of the zucchini slices over the bottom of the dish in a single layer to cover. Sprinkle with one third of the salt and pepper. Pour ⅓ cup of the heavy cream over the zucchini and sprinkle with ⅓ cup each of mozzarella cheese and fontina cheese.

Sprinkle with 2 tablespoons of Pecorino Romano cheese, then with ⅓ cup of bread crumbs. Repeat layering the ingredients two more times. (The vegetables can be assembled 8 hours ahead. Cover and refrigerate. Bring to room temperature before proceeding.) Place the baking dish on the baking sheet and bake uncovered until golden brown on top and the sauce bubbles, about 40 minutes. Serve immediately.

ROASTED BABY POTATOES
with Herbs and Garlic

I like to mix different types of potatoes for this, my all-time favorite roasted-potato recipe. The only extra time it takes is at the market, for the cashier to price a different item. Use whichever varieties you find or prefer, and serve this as a side to nearly any meat or fish dish. And it's just as easy for a crowd as it is for two people.

4 TO 6 SIDE-DISH SERVINGS

¼ cup olive oil

1 tablespoon herbes de Provence or dried Italian seasoning

3 garlic cloves, minced

1 pound fingerling potatoes or small white or red-skinned potatoes

½ pound small red-skinned potatoes (about 1¾-inch diameter)

½ pound small white-skinned potatoes (about 1¾-inch diameter)

1 teaspoon salt, plus more to taste

1 teaspoon freshly ground black pepper, plus more to taste

PREHEAT THE OVEN to 400 degrees F. In a large bowl, whisk the oil, herbes de Provence, and garlic to blend. Add all of the potatoes and 1 teaspoon each of salt and pepper, and toss to coat. Using a slotted spoon, transfer the potatoes to a large, heavy baking sheet, spacing evenly. Set the bowl aside (do not clean the bowl).

Roast the potatoes until they are tender and golden, turning them occasionally, about 1 hour. Transfer the roasted potatoes to the reserved bowl and toss to coat with any herb oil remaining in the bowl. Season the potatoes with more salt and pepper to taste. Transfer to a large bowl and serve.

Herb-Roasted
ROOT VEGETABLES

Root vegetables are particularly forgiving when it comes to roasting times: Slightly undercooked and they have a little extra firmness, while on the other hand it takes quite a while to overcook them to the mushiness point. So this recipe is one of my main choices when I'm preparing an entrée that's going to require stovetop attention at the end of cooking. While I'm reducing a sauce or sautéing some veal, I don't want to worry that I'll need to remove the veggies from the oven at precisely 7:15. And with this recipe, I don't.

6 SIDE-DISH SERVINGS

4 medium carrots (about 1 pound), peeled and cut crosswise into 1½-inch-thick slices

4 medium parsnips (about 1 pound), peeled and cut crosswise into 1½-inch-thick slices

8 ounces Brussels sprouts, halved

1 large sweet potato (about 8 ounces), peeled and cut crosswise into 1½-inch-thick slices

⅓ cup extra-virgin olive oil

1 tablespoon dried oregano

1 tablespoon dried basil

1 teaspoon dried thyme

1 teaspoon dried rosemary

2 teaspoons kosher salt, plus more to taste

2 teaspoons freshly ground black pepper, plus more to taste

POSITION THE RACK in the center of the oven and preheat the oven to 400 degrees F. In a large bowl, toss the carrots, parsnips, Brussels sprouts, sweet potato, oil, and herbs with 2 teaspoons each of kosher salt and pepper to coat. Arrange the vegetables evenly on a large, heavy baking sheet. Roast the vegetables until tender and golden, stirring occasionally, about 35 minutes. Season with more salt and pepper to taste. (The vegetables can be made up to 4 hours ahead. Rewarm in the oven before serving.) Transfer the vegetables to a platter and serve.

QUICK AND SIMPLE

Sometimes you want slow-roasted, sweet, caramelized root vegetables. But sometimes you want your veggies bright and crisp, tasting as much as possible like freshness itself. For me this is especially so in the summer; when ripe produce is at its peak, you don't want to spend a lot of time over the stove, and you're looking for a vibrant plate. These are the recipes for those times.

PEAS AND PROSCIUTTO

Perhaps you'll consider it "cheating" to add luxurious prosciutto to a vegetable dish, but I consider it a genius way to liven up the plate. And this is the easiest side dish you will ever make. I like to add this to my scrambled eggs for breakfast.

6 SIDE-DISH SERVINGS

- 2 tablespoons olive oil
- 3 shallots, chopped
- 1 garlic clove, minced
- 1 (1-pound) bag frozen peas
- 4 ounces thinly sliced prosciutto, diced
- ¼ cup chopped fresh flat-leaf parsley
- ¼ teaspoon salt, plus more to taste
- ¼ teaspoon freshly ground black pepper, plus more to taste

IN A LARGE, heavy skillet, heat the oil over a medium-low flame. Add the shallots and garlic, and sauté until tender, about 1 minute. Add the peas and sauté until heated through, about 5 minutes. Remove from the heat and stir in the prosciutto, parsley, and ¼ teaspoon each of salt and pepper. Season the mixture with more salt and pepper to taste. Transfer the mixture to a bowl and serve.

SAUTÉED BROCCOLI RABE
with Raisins and Pine Nuts

In my family, this is a traditional side during the holidays, but that's just my family—it's really perfect any time of year. The trick is to blanch the broccoli rabe in boiling water for a minute or so to get rid of some of the bitterness and partially cook it.

4 TO 6 SIDE-DISH SERVINGS

2 tablespoons pine nuts

   Salt

4 bunches (12 to 16 ounces each) of broccoli rabe (rapini)

¼ cup olive oil

3 garlic cloves, finely chopped

½ teaspoon dried crushed red pepper flakes

⅓ cup raisins

PREHEAT THE OVEN to 350 degrees F. Place the pine nuts on a heavy baking sheet, and toast in the oven until the nuts are fragrant and light golden brown, stirring once, about 7 minutes. Let cool.

Bring a large pot of salted water to a boil. Working in batches, cook the broccoli rabe in the boiling salted water until crisp-tender, about 1 minute. Transfer the blanched broccoli rabe to a large bowl of ice water to cool. Reserve ¼ cup of the cooking liquid. Drain the broccoli rabe again and set aside. (The pine nuts and broccoli rabe can be made 8 hours ahead. Store the pine nuts airtight at room temperature. Cover and refrigerate the broccoli rabe.)

In a large, heavy skillet, heat the oil over a medium flame. Add the garlic and red pepper flakes, and sauté until the garlic is golden, about 2 minutes. Add the broccoli rabe, raisins, and ¼ teaspoon of salt, and toss to coat. Add the reserved cooking liquid and cook until the broccoli rabe is heated through and the stems are tender, about 5 minutes. Season with more salt to taste. Just before serving, toss the mixture with the toasted pine nuts. Transfer to a bowl and serve.

BRUSSELS SPROUTS WITH PANCETTA

Brussels sprouts are a member of the cabbage family—and, in fact, they really do look like miniature cabbage. I think Brussels sprouts got a bad rap from the bad-cooking epidemic that seems to have swept America in the mid-twentieth-century: boiling veggies for so long that they became mushy, flavorless, and colorless. This is bad for nearly any vegetables, and particularly awful for the cabbage family, whose crisp texture (when cooked properly) is wonderful, especially when paired with the crisp, salty pancetta. Try this recipe, and see why the Belgians are proud to lend their capital's name.

4 SIDE-DISH SERVINGS

1 pound fresh Brussels sprouts, trimmed

2 tablespoons olive oil

3 ounces paper-thin slices of pancetta, coarsely chopped

2 garlic cloves, minced

¾ cup reduced-sodium chicken broth

½ teaspoon freshly ground black pepper, plus more to taste

¼ teaspoon salt, plus more to taste

BRING A LARGE POT of salted water to a boil. Add the Brussels sprouts and cook until crisp-tender, about 10 minutes. Drain. Place the Brussels sprouts in a large bowl of ice water to cool completely. Drain again. (The Brussels sprouts can be prepared up to this point 8 hours ahead. Dry thoroughly and refrigerate in a resealable plastic bag.)

Meanwhile, in a large, heavy skillet, heat the oil over a medium flame. Add the pancetta and sauté until it begins to crisp, about 5 minutes. Add the garlic and sauté until pale golden, about 2 minutes. Using a slotted spoon, transfer the pancetta mixture to a large serving bowl. Add the Brussels sprouts to the same skillet and sauté until heated through and beginning to brown, about 5 minutes. Add the broth, ½ teaspoon of pepper, and ¼ teaspoon of salt, and simmer until the broth reduces just enough to coat the Brussels sprouts, about 3 minutes.

Transfer the Brussels sprout mixture to the pancetta mixture, and toss to combine. Season with more salt and pepper to taste, and serve.

EVERYDAY CAPONATA

Caponata is one of the great Sicilian vegetable dishes, often eaten as a relish alongside pork roast or fish. The eggplant-based recipe features a wonderful sweet-and-sour taste, one of the hallmarks of Sicilian cooking—a combination of sugar and vinegar that provides a tingling push-and-pull sensation in the mouth. In my family, we often ate caponata as an antipasto, spooned over toasted bread, and used any leftovers for wonderful sandwiches. It can be eaten hot, cold, or at room temperature, making it the ultimate vegetable dish for a casual party.

6 SIDE-DISH SERVINGS

¼ cup olive oil

1 celery stalk, chopped

1 medium eggplant, cut into ½-inch cubes

1 medium onion, chopped

1 red bell pepper, cored, seeded, and cut into ½-inch pieces

1 (14½-ounce) can diced tomatoes with juices

3 tablespoons raisins

½ teaspoon dried oregano leaves

¼ cup red wine vinegar

4 teaspoons sugar

1 tablespoon drained capers

½ teaspoon salt, plus more to taste

½ teaspoon freshly ground black pepper, plus more to taste

Fresh basil leaves, for garnish

IN A LARGE, heavy skillet, heat the oil over a medium flame. Add the celery and sauté until crisp-tender, about 2 minutes. Add the eggplant and sauté until beginning to soften, about 2 minutes. Add the onion and sauté until translucent, about 3 minutes. Add the red pepper and cook until crisp-tender, about 5 minutes. Add the diced tomatoes with their juices, raisins, and oregano. Simmer over medium-low heat until the flavors blend and the mixture thickens, stirring often, about 20 minutes. Stir in the vinegar, sugar, capers, and ½ teaspoon each of salt and pepper. Season with more salt and pepper to taste. Transfer the caponata to a bowl, garnish with the basil leaves, and serve.

BROCCOLI AND GREEN BEANS

In this recipe, I blanch the broccoli before sautéing it. I love vegetables sautéed in olive oil that's fragrant with garlic, but too often, these sautés can turn fresh, crisp produce into something greasy and soggy. So for some thicker-cut vegetables like broccoli florets, the blanching step really helps: By boiling, you cook the veggies most of the way through, and then you finish with the sauté more for flavor and texture than to get the broccoli fully cooked. Less time in the oil, less chance of sogginess.

4 SIDE-DISH SERVINGS

Salt

8 cups of broccoli florets (about 2 pounds including the stems)

½ pound green beans, trimmed

½ cup extra-virgin olive oil

2 garlic cloves, thinly sliced

1½ teaspoons dried crushed red pepper flakes, plus more to taste

½ teaspoon sea salt, plus more to taste

½ teaspoon freshly ground black pepper, plus more to taste

BRING A LARGE POT of salted water to a boil. Add the broccoli and cook just until the color brightens, about 2 minutes. Using a slotted spoon, transfer the broccoli to a large bowl of ice water to cool completely. Drain the broccoli and set aside.

Cook the green beans in the same pot of boiling salted water just until the color brightens, about 4 minutes. Drain, then add the green beans to another large bowl of ice water to cool completely. (The vegetables can be prepared up to this point 8 hours ahead. Dry thoroughly and refrigerate in a resealable plastic bag.)

In a large sauté pan, heat the oil over a medium-high flame. When almost smoking, add the garlic and 1½ teaspoons of red pepper flakes, and sauté just until fragrant and the garlic is pale golden, about 45 seconds. Using a slotted spoon, remove the garlic from the oil and discard (do not overcook the garlic as it will impart a very bitter taste to the dish). Add the broccoli, green beans, and ½ teaspoon each of sea salt and black pepper to the oil, and sauté until the vegetables are heated through and crisp-tender, about 5 minutes. Season with more red pepper flakes, sea salt, and black pepper to taste. Transfer the mixture to a bowl and serve immediately.

SMASHED PARMESAN POTATOES

I love mashed potatoes as much as the next person, but most recipes take a long time—and a lot of elbow grease—to make. So I smash the unpeeled, cooked potatoes with a fork to save time, and I add olive oil and Parmesan cheese to make them rich and velvety. And that's it!

6 TO 8 SIDE-DISH SERVINGS

3 pounds red-skinned potatoes, unpeeled, quartered

2/3 cup freshly grated Parmesan cheese

1/2 cup extra-virgin olive oil

Salt and freshly ground black pepper to taste

PUT THE POTATOES in a large pot with water to cover by at least 2 inches. Cover and bring the water to a boil. Continue boiling until the potatoes are tender, about 15 minutes. Drain, reserving 3/4 cup of the cooking liquid. Return the potatoes to the pot. Coarsely mash the potatoes with a fork, adding enough of the reserved cooking liquid to moisten. Stir in the Parmesan cheese and the oil. Season to taste with salt and pepper and serve.

Feel free to use whatever vegetables are available.

GRILLED VEGETABLES

Not only do these veggies look and taste great, but they cook quickly, there's no mess, you can serve them at any temperature, and you can make them ahead of time. Plus, the leftovers can be used on sandwiches or in salads, as condiments or side dishes.

6 SIDE-DISH SERVINGS

- 3 red bell peppers, seeded and quartered
- 3 yellow squash (1 pound), cut into ½-inch-thick rounds
- 3 zucchini (12 ounces), cut into ½-inch-thick rounds
- 3 Japanese eggplants (12 ounces), cut into ½-inch-thick rounds
- 12 cremini mushrooms or button mushrooms
- 1 bunch of asparagus (about 1 pound), trimmed
- 12 green onions, trimmed
- ¼ cup plus 2 tablespoons olive oil
- 1½ teaspoons salt, plus more to taste
- 1½ teaspoons freshly ground black pepper, plus more to taste
- 3 tablespoons balsamic vinegar
- 1 garlic clove, minced
- 1 teaspoon chopped fresh flat-leaf parsley
- 1 teaspoon chopped fresh basil
- ½ teaspoon finely chopped fresh rosemary

PREPARE A CHARCOAL or gas grill for medium-high heat, or preheat a ridged grill pan over a medium-high flame. Brush the vegetables with ¼ cup of the oil to coat lightly. Sprinkle the vegetables with 1 teaspoon each of salt and pepper. Working in batches, grill the vegetables until tender and lightly charred all over, about 12 minutes for the bell peppers; 7 minutes for the yellow squash, zucchini, eggplant, and mushrooms; and 4 minutes for the asparagus and green onions. Arrange the vegetables on a platter.

In a small bowl, whisk the vinegar, garlic, parsley, basil, rosemary, the remaining 2 tablespoons of oil, and ½ teaspoon each of salt and pepper to blend. Season with more salt and pepper to taste. Drizzle the dressing over the vegetables, and serve warm or at room temperature.

Everyday
SALADS

I love vinaigrette-tossed mesclun as much as the next person does, but

you don't really need a cookbook to tell you how to do that, do you? So I

won't. To me, "salad" doesn't just mean dressed lettuce and other raw

veggies, and I like to push the envelope with flavors and textures, and

do something a little unexpected, as in these recipes.

ENDIVE AND FRISÉE SALAD
with Blood Oranges and Hazelnuts

Italians aren't afraid of using spicy and slightly bitter greens in their salads, and you shouldn't be either. Belgian endive are small, pale (white) heads of lettuce with yellow tips; they can be eaten raw (as in this salad) or grilled or roasted—the possibilities are endless. Frisée has slender, curly leaves that are a yellow-green color. The blood oranges add a hint of tart sweetness and a beautiful refreshing color to this salad—they're orange with bright red or red-streaked white flesh. The dressing, nuts, orange segments, and lettuces can all be prepared ahead of time, no last-minute fuss.

6 SIDE-DISH SERVINGS

¼ cup balsamic vinegar

2 tablespoons finely chopped shallots

1 tablespoon honey

⅓ cup olive oil or hazelnut oil

Salt and freshly ground black pepper to taste

3 heads Belgian endive, trimmed and cut crosswise into thin slices

2 heads frisée lettuce, center leaves only, torn into pieces

2 blood oranges or regular oranges, segmented

½ cup hazelnuts, toasted and chopped (see Note)

IN A MEDIUM BOWL, whisk the balsamic vinegar, shallots, and honey to blend. Gradually whisk in the oil. Season to taste with salt and pepper.

Toss the endive and frisée in a large bowl with enough vinaigrette to coat and season to taste with salt and pepper. Mound the greens on plates and surround with the orange segments. Sprinkle with the hazelnuts. Drizzle any remaining vinaigrette around the salads and serve immediately.

To toast hazelnuts, *preheat the oven to 350 degrees F. Place the nuts on a large, heavy baking sheet and toast in the oven, stirring occasionally, until they are fragrant and light golden brown in the center, about 7 minutes. Let cool completely. Rub the hazelnuts between your palms to remove their dark skins. Chop in a food processor or wrap in a kitchen towel and chop with the back of a chef's knife.*

FARRO SALAD
with Tomatoes and Herbs

Farro is a type of wheat that was an important component of the Roman Empire's diet, but it fell somewhat out of favor when more refined wheat products became plentiful in Italy. You'll still find it on a lot of Italian tables, though, and especially in soups and salads such as this one. Farro is available in Italian markets and gourmet grocery stores, but brown rice or barley could also be used in this recipe.

6 SIDE-DISH SERVINGS

10 ounces farro (about 1½ cups)

2¼ teaspoons salt, plus more to taste

1 large garlic clove, minced

2 tablespoons balsamic vinegar

¼ teaspoon freshly ground black pepper, plus more to taste

¼ cup extra-virgin olive oil

2 medium-sized tomatoes, seeded and chopped

½ medium-size sweet onion (such as Walla Walla), finely chopped

¼ cup snipped fresh chives

¼ cup finely chopped fresh flat-leaf parsley

IN A MEDIUM SAUCEPAN, combine 4 cups water and farro. Bring to a boil over high heat. Cover and simmer over medium-low heat until the farro is almost tender, about 20 minutes. Add 2 teaspoons of salt and simmer until the farro is tender, about 10 minutes longer. Drain well, then transfer to a large bowl and let cool.

In a medium bowl, mash the garlic with ¼ teaspoon of salt to make a paste. Whisk in the vinegar and ¼ teaspoon of pepper, then the oil. Add the tomatoes, onion, chives, and parsley to the farro and toss to combine. Add the vinaigrette to the salad and toss to coat. Season the salad with more salt and pepper to taste. (The salad can be made 1 day ahead. Cover and refrigerate. Bring to room temperature before serving.)

PANZANELLA

Panzanella comes from the Latin word panis, *meaning "bread." This is another dish that illustrates Italians' resourcefulness when it comes to leftovers: The key to this dish is the actually stale—not fresh—bread, which absorbs the flavors in the salad without falling apart and becoming mushy. In the sixteenth century, panzanella was made with just bread, oil, and vinegar. Tomatoes were introduced to Italy in the sixteenth century, but even then they only began to be eaten in the south, where they grew, two hundred years later. Now, of course, Italians all over the Boot love the tomato, and this salad is a staple everywhere.*

6 SIDE-DISH SERVINGS

- 6 ripe tomatoes (about 2¼ pounds total)
- 12 ounces ciabatta or other country-style white bread, 2 to 3 days old
- ⅔ cup plus 4 tablespoons extra-virgin olive oil
- ¼ cup plus 2 tablespoons red wine vinegar
- 1 garlic clove, minced
- ¾ teaspoon salt, plus more to taste
- ¾ teaspoon freshly ground black pepper, plus more to taste
- ½ cup thinly sliced fresh basil, plus whole sprigs for garnish
- ¼ cup capers, drained
- 1 cup jarred roasted red bell pepper strips, drained
- ¼ cup pitted kalamata olives, halved lengthwise

BRING A LARGE SAUCEPAN of water to a boil. Prepare a large bowl of ice water. Cut an X at the bottom of each tomato and submerge the tomatoes in the boiling water for 10 seconds. Using a slotted spoon, transfer the tomatoes to the ice water to cool slightly. Using a small, sharp paring knife, peel off the tomato skins and cut the tomatoes in half. Scoop out and discard the seeds, then cut the tomatoes into 1-inch cubes.

Cut the crusts off the bread, and cut or tear the bread into 1-inch cubes. In a large bowl, whisk ⅔ cup of oil, ¼ cup of vinegar, the garlic, and ½ teaspoon each of salt and pepper to blend. Add the bread cubes, tomatoes, and sliced basil, and toss to combine. Set aside until the bread absorbs the vinaigrette, tossing occasionally, about 5 minutes. Season the salad with more salt and pepper to taste.

In a small bowl, soak the capers in the remaining 2 tablespoons of vinegar for 10 minutes. Drain. In another small bowl toss the roasted peppers with 2 tablespoons of the oil. Season the peppers with $\frac{1}{4}$ teaspoon each of salt and pepper.

Transfer half of the bread mixture to a $13 \times 9 \times 2$-inch glass dish. Arrange half of the roasted peppers, capers, and olives over the bread mixture. Repeat layering with the remaining bread mixture, then the remaining peppers, capers, and olives. Cover the salad and let stand at room temperature for the flavors to blend, at least 1 hour and up to 4 hours.

Drizzle the remaining 2 tablespoons of oil over the salad. Garnish with the basil sprigs and serve.

Here are a couple *of other great uses for stale bread: To make bread crumbs, cut the stale bread into pieces, then place them in the bowl of a food processor and pulse until they're finely ground. To make croutons, cut the stale bread into bite-size pieces, then place them on a baking sheet and drizzle with olive oil. Bake in a preheated 350 degree F oven until crisp and golden, about 8 minutes.*

everyday

dolci

EVERYDAY FRUIT

Fruit Salad with Cannoli Cream ▪ Grilled Peaches with Mascarpone Cheese ▪ Peaches Stuffed with Amaretti Cookies ▪ Cantaloupe, Strawberries, and Grapes with White Wine and Mint ▪ Marinated Strawberries over Pound Cake ▪ Grilled Pineapple with Nutella

EVERYDAY CREAMS AND PUDDINGS

Affogato ▪ Chocolate Zabaglione ▪ Chocolate Tiramisù ▪ Rice Pudding with Vanilla, Orange, and Rum ▪ Panna Cotta with Fresh Berries

EVERYDAY COOKIES AND CAKES

Almond Cake ▪ Chocolate Amaretti Cake ▪ Citrus Biscotti ▪ Pine Nut Cookies ▪ Toasted Pound Cake with Mascarpone and Amaretto

Everyday
FRUIT

Italians love fruit for dessert, and not just in the time-consuming and fattening pies and tarts that are so popular here in the United States. In Italy, fruit—like many ingredients—is often treated more simply: grilled or poached, raw or baked, with drizzles of this or dashes of that. If you can make any generalization about Italian fruit desserts, it's that their recipes let the fresh flavors of the fruit itself do all the work, instead of relying on butter, sugar, and flour. Of course, this puts a higher burden on the fruit: If you're not dousing it in sugar and surrounding it with buttery batter, it has to be that much better. So seasonality is key: While you might bake an off-season peach into a cobbler, you're not going to want to grill it to serve with mascarpone.

FRUIT SALAD
with Cannoli Cream

Cannoli ("pipes") are said to be one of the unshakable rocks of Sicilian desserts, and these days they can be found in almost every Italian pastry shop in America. They are crispy fried pastry tubes that are filled with sweetened ricotta cheese or sometimes pastry cream. The tubes are time-consuming to make, but the filling is easy, and dolloped over fresh berries, well, it just brings me home.

4 SERVINGS

⅓ cup whole-milk ricotta cheese

2 tablespoons plus ⅓ cup whipping cream

3 tablespoons powdered sugar

Pinch of ground cinnamon

12 ounces fresh strawberries, hulled and quartered (about 2½ cups)

½ pint fresh raspberries (about 1¼ cups)

1 tablespoon sugar

1 tablespoon fresh lemon juice

2 kiwi, peeled and cut into ½-inch pieces

3 tablespoons sliced almonds, toasted

IN A MEDIUM BOWL, stir the ricotta and 2 tablespoons of cream to blend. In a large bowl using an electric mixer, beat the remaining ⅓ cup of cream with the powdered sugar and cinnamon until semi-firm peaks form. Fold the ricotta into the whipped cream. (This mixture can be prepared up to 4 hours ahead. Cover and refrigerate.)

In a medium bowl, toss the strawberries, raspberries, sugar, and lemon juice to combine. Let stand until juices form, tossing occasionally, about 20 minutes. Add the kiwi and toss gently.

Spoon the fruit mixture into 4 dessert bowls. Dollop the ricotta cream atop the fruit, sprinkle with the almonds, and serve.

GRILLED PEACHES
with Mascarpone Cheese

In the summer, I like to buy large bags or baskets of fresh peaches at the farmers' market. I eat the perfectly ripe ones immediately and use the firmer (but still ripe) specimens for this amazing dessert combo. But do be sure that your peaches are a little firm; if they're going soft all over, they'll fall apart on the grill. Add the cheese mixture right before you serve it so it looks fresh.

2 tablespoons sugar

2 tablespoons brandy

1 tablespoon fresh lemon juice

Olive oil

3 firm but ripe peaches, pitted and quartered

½ cup mascarpone cheese, at room temperature

¼ teaspoon pure vanilla extract

¾ cup dry white wine

STIR THE SUGAR, brandy, and lemon juice in a medium bowl to blend. Set the brandy mixture aside.

Prepare a charcoal or gas grill for medium-high heat, or preheat a ridged grill pan over a medium-high flame. Lightly brush the grill rack or pan with oil. Grill the peaches until they are heated through and beginning to brown, turning occasionally, about 5 minutes. Immediately transfer the grilled peaches to the brandy mixture, and toss to coat. Set aside for 15 minutes, tossing occasionally.

Meanwhile, in a small bowl, stir the mascarpone and vanilla to blend.

Divide the peach mixture equally among 6 coupe dishes and pour the wine over the peaches. Dollop the mascarpone mixture atop the peaches, and serve.

PEACHES STUFFED
with Amaretti Cookies

Amaretti cookies are a must for this recipe; there really isn't any substitute for that crunchy almond flavor and texture. They're becoming more and more popular and easier to find, especially in Italian specialty stores, and they last for a long time; so when you find them, stock up.

6 SERVINGS

⅓ cup cold whipping cream

4 teaspoons unsalted butter

12 small amaretti cookies (Italian macaroons; about 1½ ounces total)

3 ripe but firm peaches (about 5 ounces each), halved and pitted

3 teaspoons sugar

IN A MEDIUM BOWL, beat the cream with an electric mixer until soft peaks form. Cover and refrigerate the whipped cream until ready to use.

Preheat the oven to 375 degrees F. Spread 1 teaspoon of butter over the bottom of an 8-inch baking dish. In the bowl of a food processor, pulse the amaretti cookies until finely crumbled. Using a melon baller, scoop out the red flesh from the center of each peach. Arrange the peaches cut side up in the prepared dish. Fill the center of the peaches with the amaretti cookie crumbs. Dot each peach with ½ teaspoon of butter, then sprinkle ½ teaspoon of sugar over each. (The whipped cream and peaches can be prepared 4 hours ahead. Keep the whipped cream refrigerated. Cover and refrigerate the peaches.)

Bake the peaches until they are tender and the filling is crisp on top, about 30 minutes. Serve warm with the whipped cream.

CANTALOUPE, STRAWBERRIES,
and Grapes with
White Wine and Mint

This recipe was born out of leftovers—a half cantaloupe, a handful of straw-berries, some grapes—not enough in themselves to feed a family, but com-bine them and you have a great dessert. Feel free to substitute with your favorite fruit or whatever you happen to have as leftovers. The sweetened wine and the fresh mint meld the fruit flavors together into a wonderfully refreshing, quick, and easy recipe. Perfect for summertime.

4 SERVINGS

1¼   cups dry white wine

⅓   cup sugar

 1   tablespoon chopped fresh mint

½   ripe cantaloupe, halved, seeded, and cut into ¾-inch cubes
    (about 3 cups)

 1   (8-ounce) basket of fresh strawberries, quartered

 1   cup seedless green grapes, halved lengthwise

IN A SMALL SAUCEPAN, bring the wine and sugar to a boil, stirring until the sugar is dissolved. Boil for 2 minutes. Remove from the heat and stir in the mint.

In a large bowl, combine the cantaloupe, strawberries, and grapes. Pour the warm wine mixture over and toss to coat. Cover and refrigerate until cold, stirring occasionally, at least 2 hours and up to 8 hours.

Transfer the fruit mixture to serving bowls and serve chilled.

MARINATED STRAWBERRIES
over Pound Cake

One word: easy. Make that two: delicious.

4 SERVINGS

- 1 quart fresh strawberries, hulled and halved
- ⅓ cup aged balsamic vinegar
- About 1 to 2 tablespoons sugar
- ⅓ cup cold whipping cream
- 4 slices fresh pound cake (each slice ½ inch thick)
- ⅓ cup amaretto liqueur
- 6 amaretti cookies (Italian macaroons), crumbled (optional)

IN A SMALL, shallow casserole dish, toss the strawberries and vinegar, and let stand at room temperature for 20 minutes. Sweeten the strawberry mixture with enough sugar to taste.

In a medium bowl, beat the cream with an electric mixer until soft peaks form. Cover and refrigerate the whipped cream until ready to use. (The whipped cream can be made 4 hours ahead. Keep refrigerated.)

Place 1 slice of pound cake on each of 4 plates. Brush the amaretto liqueur over the cake slices. Spoon the strawberry mixture over. Top each with a large dollop of whipped cream. Sprinkle the amaretti crumbs over, if desired, and serve.

Although canned pineapple wouldn't be my first choice, you can use it if you pat the slices dry before grilling.

GRILLED PINEAPPLE
with Nutella

Pineapple doesn't quite qualify as Italian, but Nutella (a chocolate-hazelnut spread) is definitely an Italian favorite of cult-like proportions, so this can certainly pass as an Italian-American recipe. Grilling the pineapple enhances its sweet flavor, provides the great grill marks, and of course warms it up, bringing a new level of comfort to this incredibly comforting dessert.

6 SERVINGS

¼ cup hazelnuts

¼ teaspoon pure vanilla extract

⅓ cup mascarpone cheese

⅓ cup chocolate-hazelnut spread (such as Nutella)

3 tablespoons whipping cream

Olive oil

1 pineapple, peeled and cut crosswise into ½-inch-thick slices

PREHEAT THE OVEN to 350 degrees F. Place the hazelnuts on a large, heavy baking sheet, and toast in the oven, stirring occasionally, until the nuts are fragrant and light golden brown in the center, about 7 minutes. Let cool completely. Rub the hazelnuts between your palms to remove the dark skins from the nuts. Chop the hazelnuts and set aside.

In a small bowl, stir the vanilla into the mascarpone just to blend. Set aside. In another small bowl, combine the chocolate-hazelnut spread and the cream. Microwave until warm, stirring every 20 seconds to blend, about 1 minute total.

Prepare a charcoal or gas grill for medium-high heat, or preheat a ridged grill pan over a medium-high flame. Lightly oil the grill rack or pan. Grill the pineapple slices until heated through and beginning to brown, about 3 minutes per side.

Transfer the pineapple slices to a large platter, and drizzle the warm chocolate-hazelnut sauce over. Dollop the mascarpone mixture atop. Sprinkle with the hazelnuts and serve.

CREAMS AND PUDDINGS

These are the rich, traditional finales that I remember from big family suppers when I was growing up—and that you may recognize from the menus of many Italian restaurants. While some of these aren't as simple as just grilling peaches, they're still not very complicated, and doubling or tripling these recipes is a piece of cake (so to speak), making them perfect for your own big family suppers.

AFFOGATO

This dessert is the Italian version of a hot fudge sundae. Traditionally it's made with vanilla ice cream, but I love chocolate, so why not?

4 SERVINGS

⅓ cup cold whipping cream

½ cup boiling water

1 tablespoon espresso powder

1 pint chocolate gelato or ice cream

IN A MEDIUM BOWL, beat the cream with an electric mixer until soft peaks form. Cover and refrigerate the whipped cream until ready to use. (The whipped cream can be made 4 hours ahead. Keep refrigerated.)

In a 1-cup glass measuring cup, whisk the boiling water and espresso powder until the powder is dissolved. Scoop the gelato or ice cream into 4 dessert bowls or glasses. Pour 2 tablespoons of hot espresso over each, top with the whipped cream, and serve immediately.

CHOCOLATE ZABAGLIONE

The traditional zabaglione isn't made with chocolate, but it is served either warm or cold, with fresh berries, as mine is. So why did I add chocolate? To make this something so incredibly rich and special that no one—absolutely no one—could resist it. Serve this before asking for a really big favor.

6 SERVINGS

¼ cup whipping cream

½ cup semisweet chocolate chips

⅔ cup sugar

⅔ cup dry Marsala

8 large egg yolks

Pinch of salt

1 pound fresh strawberries, hulled and quartered

IN A SMALL, heavy saucepan, bring the cream just to a simmer over medium-high heat. Remove from the heat and add the chocolate chips. Stir until the chocolate is melted and smooth. Set aside and keep warm.

Fill a large saucepan with enough water to come 2 inches up the sides of the pan, and bring to a simmer. In a large metal bowl, whisk the sugar, Marsala, egg yolks, and salt to blend. Set the bowl over the saucepan of simmering water (do not allow the bottom of the bowl to touch the water). Whisk the egg mixture constantly until it is thick and creamy and a thermometer inserted into the mixture registers 160 degrees F, about 4 minutes. Remove from the heat.

Using a large rubber spatula, fold the chocolate mixture into the egg mixture. (If serving the zabaglione cold, cover and refrigerate it until cold, at least 8 hours and up to 1 day. Do not rewarm.)

Divide the strawberries among 6 coupe dishes. Spoon the warm zabaglione over and serve.

CHOCOLATE TIRAMISÙ

It looks complicated, but all the steps are actually easy, and it will be such a hit. I like to make tiramisù the day before so that the cookies have enough time to absorb all the flavors and the tiramisù has time to set. Tiramisù means "pick-me-up," and boy oh boy will it pick you up.

12 SERVINGS

1 (8-ounce) container mascarpone cheese

¾ cup whipping cream

⅔ cup sugar

Chocolate Zabaglione (page 234), cold (½ of the recipe)

2½ cups espresso, cold

32 Savoiardi (crisp ladyfinger cookies; from two 7-ounce packages)

Unsweetened cocoa powder, for sifting

IN A LARGE BOWL, stir the mascarpone cheese two times or just until smooth (do not overmix or the mascarpone will become stiff). In a medium bowl, beat the cream and ⅓ cup of the sugar with an electric mixer until soft peaks form. Fold the sweetened whipped cream into the mascarpone, then fold in the chocolate zabaglione. Cover and refrigerate.

Line a 9¼ × 5 × 2¾-inch metal loaf pan with plastic wrap, allowing the plastic to extend over the sides. In another medium bowl, whisk the espresso and the remaining ⅓ cup of sugar to blend.

Working with one cookie at a time, dip 8 cookies into the espresso, and arrange in a single layer side by side over the bottom of the prepared pan. Spoon one third of the mascarpone mixture over the cookies to cover. Repeat the dipping and layering of the cookies and remaining mascarpone mixture two more times. Dip the remaining 8 cookies in the espresso and arrange side by side atop the tiramisù. Press lightly to compact slightly (the last layer will extend above the pan sides). Cover the tiramisù with plastic and refrigerate for at least 2 hours and up to 1 day.

Unwrap the plastic from atop the tiramisù. Invert the tiramisù onto a platter and remove the plastic. Sift the cocoa over the tiramisù and serve.

RICE PUDDING
with Vanilla, Orange, and Rum

The addition of orange and rum are what makes this a very different rice pudding than you're probably used to. Of course, rum isn't a typical flavoring in Italian cooking, but once again I've taken the liberty of infusing a little New World twist into an Old World classic.

4 TO 6 SERVINGS

5 cups whole milk

⅔ cup Arborio rice or medium-grain white rice

1 vanilla bean, split lengthwise

½ cup sugar

2 teaspoons dark rum

1 teaspoon grated orange zest

   Orange segments

IN A HEAVY, medium saucepan, combine the milk and rice. Scrape in the seeds from the vanilla bean and add the bean. Bring the milk to a boil. Reduce the heat to medium and simmer, stirring frequently, until the rice is tender, about 25 minutes. Stir in the sugar, rum, and orange zest. Cook until the mixture thickens, about 10 minutes longer. Discard the vanilla bean and spoon the rice pudding into bowls. Cover and refrigerate until the pudding is cold, about 5 hours and up to 1 day ahead. Serve with orange segments.

PANNA COTTA
with Fresh Berries

A great dinner-party dessert: You make it ahead of time, it looks beautiful, and it tastes fantastic. For an interesting twist, try infusing the cream with flavors like lavender or rosewater.

6 SERVINGS

- 1 cup whole milk
- 1 tablespoon unflavored powdered gelatin
- 3 cups whipping cream
- ⅓ cup honey
- 1 tablespoon sugar
- Pinch of salt
- 2 cups assorted fresh berries

PLACE THE MILK in a heavy, small saucepan. Sprinkle the gelatin over and let stand for 5 minutes to soften the gelatin. Stir over medium heat just until the gelatin dissolves but the milk does not boil, about 5 minutes. Add the cream, honey, sugar, and salt and stir until the sugar dissolves, about 2 minutes. Remove from the heat and let cool slightly. Pour the cream mixture into 6 wine glasses, dividing equally. Cover and refrigerate until set, at least 6 hours and up to 2 days.

Spoon the berries atop the panna cotta and serve.

Everyday
COOKIES AND CAKES

In pastas and salads and sauces and stews, it's obvious that Italian cuisine is heavily focused on the regional produce grown throughout the peninsula: The olive oil from the neighboring field is drizzled on the grilled fish from the port down the road, the fig tree in the backyard provides the sauce for the pork roast from the farmer next door. This is true for desserts also—and not just for the likes of grilled fruits, but even in cookies and cakes. The regional nuts, citrus, and even such produce as fennel play a role in Italian baked goods. Here are some of them.

ALMOND CAKE

Il Fornaio bakery in Los Angeles made a recipe for almond cake that I fell in love with many years ago. I've changed their recipe a bit to create a different texture, but the pronounced almond flavor remains the same. It's very important to cream the butter and almond paste until it becomes thoroughly smooth.

MAKES 1 (8-INCH) ROUND CAKE

½ cup fine yellow cornmeal

½ cup cake flour

1 teaspoon baking powder

½ cup (1 stick) unsalted butter, at room temperature

¼ cup almond paste, cut into small pieces

½ teaspoon pure vanilla extract

1¼ cups confectioners' sugar, plus more for dusting

4 large egg yolks

2 large eggs

¼ cup sour cream

POSITION THE RACK in the center of the oven and preheat the oven to 350 degrees F. Butter and flour an 8-inch round cake pan.

In a medium bowl, whisk together the cornmeal, cake flour, and baking powder. Using a stand mixer with a paddle attachment, beat the butter and almond paste on high speed until smooth, about 3 minutes. Reduce the speed to low and beat in the vanilla extract. Gradually add 1¼ cups of confectioners' sugar, beating until the mixture is light and fluffy, about 3 minutes. Increase the speed to high and beat in the egg yolks and whole eggs, one at a time. Reduce the speed to medium and add the sour cream and dry ingredients and mix until just incorporated.

Pour the batter into the prepared cake pan and smooth the surface with a spatula. Bake until the cake is golden and pulls away from the sides of the pan, about 35 minutes. Transfer the pan to a wire rack and let cool. Remove the cake from the pan and dust with more confectioners' sugar. (The cake can be made 1 day ahead. Store airtight in a plastic container.) Cut the cake into wedges and serve.

CHOCOLATE AMARETTI CAKE

Amaretti is strictly translated as "little bitters," but colloquially it refers to light, airy, crunchy, dome-shaped almond cookies. The cookies are great on their own, but I also love them as an ingredient in a cake; the soft cake batter and the crunchy cookie provide a wonderful contrast. So when you can't decide whether to have cookies or cake, just have both.

6 SERVINGS

Butter-flavored nonstick cooking spray

¾ cup semisweet chocolate chips

1 cup slivered almonds

1 cup (about 2 ounces) baby amaretti cookies

½ cup unsalted butter (1 stick), at room temperature

⅔ cup sugar

2 teaspoons grated orange zest (from approximately 1 orange)

4 large eggs

About 2 tablespoons unsweetened cocoa powder, for sifting

PREHEAT THE OVEN to 350 degrees F. Spray a 9-inch springform pan with nonstick spray and refrigerate.

In a small bowl, microwave the chocolate chips, stirring every 30 seconds, until melted and smooth, about 2 minutes.

In a food processor, combine the almonds and cookies, and pulse until finely ground. Transfer to a bowl. Add the butter, sugar, and orange zest to the processor and blend until creamy and smooth. With the machine running, add the eggs one at a time. Add the nut mixture and the melted chocolate. Pulse until blended.

Pour the batter into the prepared pan. Bake until the center puffs and a tester inserted into the center of the cake comes out clean, about 35 minutes. Cool the cake in the pan for 15 minutes. Transfer to a platter, sift the cocoa powder over, and serve.

CITRUS BISCOTTI

Biscotti means "twice baked," a cooking method that results in the firm, crunchy cookies that have recently become wildly popular here in America. These cookies were eaten by sailors back in Columbus's day because they last for a long time without going bad. They're great for dunking in coffee or tea, which is how my mom, nonna, and I would eat them when I was growing up. The citrus zests provide an extra little zing, and really evoke the tastes of Italy. If you want, you could use just orange or lemon; it doesn't have to be both.

MAKES 3 DOZEN COOKIES

2 cups all-purpose flour

¾ cup fine yellow cornmeal

1½ teaspoons baking powder

1 teaspoon salt

1 cup sugar

3 large eggs

1 tablespoon grated orange zest (from about 1 orange)

1 tablespoon grated lemon zest (from about 2 lemons)

½ cup coarsely chopped shelled pistachios

PREHEAT THE OVEN to 325 degrees F. Line a large baking sheet with parchment paper or a Silpat baking mat. In a large bowl, whisk together the flour, cornmeal, baking powder, and salt. In another large bowl, beat the sugar and eggs with an electric mixer until pale yellow and fluffy, about 3 minutes. Mix in the orange and lemon zests, then the flour mixture, and beat just until blended; the dough will be soft and sticky. Stir in the pistachios. Let stand for 5 minutes.

Using a rubber spatula, transfer the dough to the prepared baking sheet, forming two equal mounds spaced evenly apart. Moisten your hands with water and shape the dough into two 11 × 4-inch logs. Bake until the logs are lightly browned, about 35 minutes. Cool for 5 minutes. Using a serrated knife, cut the logs crosswise into ½-inch-thick diagonal slices. Arrange the biscotti cut side down on the same baking sheet, and bake until the cookies are pale golden, about 25 minutes. Let cool before serving.

PINE NUT COOKIES

Pine nuts and fennel seed aren't necessarily ingredients you expect to find in cookies—really, they sound much more like they're going into a pesto—but they're the secret flavors in this buttery, flaky shortbread dough that will melt in your mouth. Ground fennel seed isn't as easy to find as the whole seeds, so buy them whole and grind them at home in a mortar and pestle or coffee/spice grinder. I like to make this dough ahead of time and freeze it, then bake it off as needed.

MAKES ABOUT 3 DOZEN COOKIES

½   cup (1 stick) unsalted butter, at room temperature

½   cup plus 2 tablespoons sugar

1   teaspoon pure vanilla extract

1   teaspoon ground fennel seed

¼   teaspoon salt

1   large egg

1¼ cups all-purpose flour

¼   cup pine nuts

IN A LARGE BOWL, beat the butter, sugar, vanilla, ground fennel seed, and salt with an electric mixer until light and fluffy. Beat in the egg. Add the flour and mix just until blended.

Transfer the dough to a sheet of plastic wrap and shape into an 8-inch-long log. Wrap the dough in plastic and refrigerate for 2 hours.

Preheat the oven to 350 degrees F. Line 2 heavy, large baking sheets with parchment paper.

Cut the dough log crosswise into ⅛- to ¼-inch-thick slices. Transfer the cookies to the prepared baking sheets, spacing evenly apart. Press the pine nuts decoratively atop the cookies, and bake until the cookies are golden around the edges, about 15 minutes. (The cookies can be made 1 day ahead. Store airtight at room temperature.)

TOASTED POUND CAKE
with Mascarpone and Amaretto

So this, my finale, is the ultimate in Everyday Italian *cooking. Sure, there's some cheating involved—I'm not asking you to bake a pound cake. But this distinct combination of Italian flavors will transport you to a piazza-side café, nibbling this great dessert, sipping espressos, and people-watching, instead of struggling in the kitchen for hours upon end. That's been my goal in this book. I hope I've succeeded.*

6 SERVINGS

¼ cup sliced almonds

¾ cup apricot preserves

3 tablespoons amaretto liqueur

1 (10.75-ounce) pound cake, cut crosswise into 12 slices

⅔ cup mascarpone cheese

PREHEAT THE OVEN to 350 degrees F. Place the almonds on a large, heavy baking sheet, and toast in the oven, stirring occasionally, until the nuts are fragrant and light golden brown, about 7 minutes. Let cool completely.

In a small bowl, stir the apricot preserves and amaretto to blend. Working in batches, toast the pound cake slices in a toaster until golden.

Place 1 cake slice atop each of six plates, and spoon the mascarpone cheese atop the cake slices. Arrange the remaining cake slices offset atop the bottom cake slices. Spoon the apricot mixture over. Sprinkle with the almonds and serve immediately.

You could also grill the pound cake or toast it

in the oven—whatever is easier.

Many Thanks

I'm indebted to my family, who have always inspired me to achieve great things, and of course for passing along the passion for food and family. My mother, for financing and supporting my culinary education and for all the love and support over the years—thanks. My Aunt Raffy, for sharing family recipe secrets and for all the fun we have cooking together—priceless. To my sister, Eloisa, my brother Igor, and my best friend, Jen—thank you for all your support and love.

To all the wonderful and talented people who helped create this cookbook and bring it to life. A special thanks to Victoria Pearson, the most gifted photographer I know, and Rori Trovato, a brilliant food stylist. Julie Clevering, the best darn makeup artist. Rochelle Palermo, for always being upbeat and positive about testing and retesting recipes—you are such a pleasure to work with. Eric Greenspan, my friend and lawyer (and manager), for always looking out for me. My editor, Chris Pavone at Clarkson Potter, who guided me so brilliantly and was so patient.

A special thanks to Anthropologie for being so generous and outfitting me.

To the Food Network for giving me the chance to share my love of Italian food and family with *sooo* many people. Bob Tuschman, who brought me to the Food Network family and who believed in me from the start—many thanks. Irene Wong, who is not only my producer (on *Everyday Italian*) but has become a wonderful friend—thank you for all your hard work and dedication. And a *big* thanks to the *Everyday Italian* team for all their hard work and for making my job so much fun.

And to Mario Batali: Thanks for all the great advice, my friend.

Index

Conversion Chart

American cooks use standard containers, the 8-ounce cup and a tablespoon that takes exactly 16 level fillings to fill that cup level. Measuring by cup makes it very difficult to give weight equivalents, as a cup of densely packed butter will weigh considerably more than a cup of flour. The easiest way therefore to deal with cup measurements in recipes is to take the amount by volume rather than by weight. Thus the equation reads:

1 cup = 240 ml = 8 fl. oz.   ½ cup = 120 ml = 4 fl. oz.

It is possible to buy a set of American cup measures in major stores around the world.

In the States, butter is often measured in sticks. One stick is the equivalent of 8 tablespoons. One tablespoon of butter is therefore the equivalent to ½ ounce/15 grams.

LIQUID MEASURES

FLUID OUNCES	U.S.	IMPERIAL	MILLILITERS
	1 teaspoon	1 teaspoon	5
¼	2 teaspoons	1 dessertspoon	10
½	1 tablespoon	1 tablespoon	14
1	2 tablespoons	2 tablespoons	28
2	¼ cup	4 tablespoons	56
4	½ cup		120
5		¼ pint or 1 gill	140
6	¾ cup		170
8	1 cup		240
9			250, ¼ liter
10	1¼ cups	½ pint	280
12	1½ cups		340
15		¾ pint	420
16	2 cups		450
18	2¼ cups		500, ½ liter
20	2½ cups	1 pint	560
24	3 cups		675
25		1¼ pints	700
27	3½ cups		750
30	3¾ cups	1½ pints	840
32	4 cups or 1 quart		900
35		1¾ pints	980
36	4½ cups		1000, 1 liter
40	5 cups	2 pints or 1 quart	1120

SOLID MEASURES

U.S. and Imperial Measures		Metric Measures	
OUNCES	POUNDS	GRAMS	KILOS
1		28	
2		56	
3½		100	
4	¼	112	
5		140	
6		168	
8	½	225	
9		250	¼
12	¾	340	
16	1	450	
18		500	½
20	1¼	560	
24	1½	675	
27		750	¾
28	1¾	780	
32	2	900	
36	2¼	1000	1
40	2½	1100	
48	3	1350	
54		1500	1½

OVEN TEMPERATURE EQUIVALENTS

FAHRENHEIT	CELSIUS	GAS MARK	DESCRIPTION
225	110	¼	Cool
250	130	½	
275	140	1	Very Slow
300	150	2	
325	170	3	Slow
350	180	4	Moderate
375	190	5	
400	200	6	Moderately Hot
425	220	7	Fairly Hot
450	230	8	Hot
475	240	9	Very Hot
500	250	10	Extremely Hot

Any broiling recipes can be used with the grill of the oven, but beware of high-temperature grills.

EQUIVALENTS FOR INGREDIENTS

all-purpose flour—plain flour
coarse salt—kitchen salt
cornstarch—cornflour
eggplant—aubergine

half and half—12% fat milk
heavy cream—double cream
light cream—single cream
lima beans—broad beans

scallion—spring onion
unbleached flour—strong, white flour
zest—rind
zucchini—courgettes or marrow